MW01621058

DISTILLERY Finance

Maria Pearman

White Mule Press, a division of
American Distilling Institute
PO Box 577
Hayward, CA 94541
distilling.com/publications/books

ISBN 978-1-7369802-6-2

TABLE OF CONTENTS

Acknowledgements

This book marks my second time around the block with a publication. The process hasn't gotten easier, nor has the joy of compiling information for the reader diminished. Many distilleries begin with the founder's appreciation for the craft, but the finances are often an afterthought. I aspire to help distillery owners and operators understand the forces of their business in hopes that, armed with this knowledge, they can bring more of their excellence into the world.

As with my previous book, Small Brewery Finance, many industry professionals contributed content. They shared their stories, from tales of luck getting into the industry at the right time, to descriptions of rigorous corporate discipline and a dogged determination to succeed. Thank you Ryan Thompson, Alan Dietrich, Chris Joseph, Jon Gostnell. Distillery industry service providers chimed in with words of wisdom, allowing us to learn through their experience. I'm grateful for your contribution Peter Whalen, Marcus Reed, Shauna Barnes, and Quinton Jay.

Many hands contributed behind the scenes, offering their time to edit a chapter or provide pointers on how the information might be framed differently to better resonate with the reader. This book has been supported and improved with their participation. Thank you Rob Cassell, Jennah Padilla, Nancy McDonald.

Writing *Distillery Finance* was a unique opportunity for me to collaborate with family. My aunt Tish Anderson served as proofreader for the text. A lifelong English teacher, she is now retired. At 80 years old she fills her day with Spanish lessons, working on political campaigns she supports, and volunteering for the community. I'm not sure where she found the time to proofread these many pages, but I am honored that she did. And she taught me much along the way! What a wonderful gift to work closely with my aunt, who is a model for living life to the fullest. I am grateful for the opportunity and her generosity of time.

Preface

Of the many reasons one begins a spirits business, "to build a sustainable business" is often far down the list — if it appears at all. Many people start a distillery out of passion and learn the business side along the way. Creative entrepreneurs forge forth because they are passionate about spirits, not for a love of tracking the finances of the organization. But let's be honest, a healthy company — of any industry — must have a strong financial foundation.

Distilleries require significant financial investment and a tolerance to navigate the many rules of a highly regulated industry. Many spirits are aged products that take years to mature, and consumer preferences change more rapidly than the production cycle. It's a bit of a gamble to time the release of products to align with market trends. Add to this the increasingly competitive environment, fueled by the dramatic growth of distilleries in the U.S. According to the American Distilling Institute, in 2006 there were 75 craft distilleries in the United States; in 2021 there were 2,250. Astonishing growth.

At the same time, it's important to be nimble. Business leaders must be ready to change direction on short notice, which requires a combination of short-term planning with long-range sensibilities. Successful producers review their financial position and forecast on a daily basis. The more volatile the environment, the more frequently oversight is needed. Every distiller must model different scenarios, and always have two or three alternative courses of action ready to go. Success means being proactive, being nimble, seizing opportunity, and being willing to make hard choices.

Distilleries face a particularly challenging position: to build a business requires a lot of money and time (if making aged spirits), yet you have to be able to adapt rapidly in a dynamic environment. The more money that a business has tied up in long term projects, the more difficult it is to adjust course quickly. For these reasons it is incredibly important to have a keen understanding of corporate finance and well-organized data that allows leaders to quickly make decisions.

There is much uncertainty in the world today. Ways of doing business that felt predictable just a few years ago now change faster than we can keep up with. For business owners in the beverage alcohol industry, it's no longer good enough to react to industry activity — to be a contender, anticipate where the industry is going before it moves there. *Distillery Finance* gives owners and operators an overview of finance knowledge so that they can make better decisions for their company.

Years ago, I worked as a tax preparer in a CPA firm that served businesses from all industries; by the luck of the draw I was assigned to work on a few beverage alcohol tax returns. I saw producers spend more money having the CPA firm clean up the books at the end of the year than the cost of the tax return itself. This meant that business owners had little to no insight to their company's performance through the year. I saw an opportunity. The market needed an accountant who could help these businesses organize their financials, and who could help the owners interpret the financial results on a regular basis.

Thus, an idea was born. I started an accounting firm that offered contract Controller services specifically focused on beverage alcohol companies. The services that my firm offered eventually grew to include bookkeeping, payroll preparation, contract Controller services, and tax preparation with a niche focus in beverage alcohol. When I began the company I was an accounting generalist who happened to be working to a number of clients in the same industry. But as time went on, I learned more about the beverage alcohol operations and environment, and I observed that as my knowledge and awareness of the space grew, so too did the value of the services I was offering the client. After years of niche-focused experience, I am convinced that the more attuned to a client's operations a service provider is, the better business partner he or she can be to the client.

My personal mission has evolved to educate owner/operators within the beverage alcohol industries about financial health. To that end, the purpose of *Distillery Finance* is to be a resource for small distillery operators. This book provides a basic overview of accounting through the lens of the spirits industry. There are unique aspects of the industry that require special consideration or understanding, which one doesn't encounter in a general accounting overview. My goal is to provide enough of an education that the operator is empowered to run his or her distillery as a business, not as a hobby. The owner will have the knowledge to develop a strong foundation from which a flexible and resilient distillery can grow.

Distillery Finance covers accounting basics — from debits and credits, through an explanation of each financial report. It also covers finance theory and different options for funding the start, growth, and continuance of your business. I've included an overview of legal structure and tax characteristics for different kinds of entities. The entire content is written through a distiller's lens — that is, I highlight content of particular interest to distilleries, provide industry-relevant benchmarks, and include stories from professionals in the industry. I've also provided key checklists and templates, including a sample Chart of Accounts and sample Month-End Close Checklist.

Now is the moment for *Distillery Finance* because the industry is growing rapidly. We are seeing more and more distilleries open, and there few resources for financial management that focus on this space. My goal is to take away barriers for producers so that they can bring more of their excellence into the world. I hope that the content of *Distillery Finance* will help spirits producers to create a financially sustainable business that allows them to continue to let excellence shine for years to come.

CHAPTER **ONE**

Introduction to Financial Management

"Accounting is the language of business" is often the first statement from an Accounting 101 professor. How many of us recall sitting through that opening line, convinced we would never use these principles in the real world? Admittedly clichéd, the words are quite true. Accounting *is* a language, and this chapter introduces some of the basic structure, syntax, and terms. If accounting seems dry and one-dimensional, it may help to pause for a moment to appreciate its wonderfully organized structure.

***AUTHOR'S NOTE:** One of my mentors once raved about the beauty of partnership tax law. How the intricacies of its rules is like poetry! I will not go as far as to suggest that accounting is art, but I must agree — it has a certain lovely balance.*

Language has components that build on each other. Letters are grouped into words; words into sentences, and sentences into paragraphs. Similarly, accounting has transactions, account ledgers, and a general ledger.

An accounting transaction is the smallest unit of the accounting language. In each transaction there are two sides: a debit and a credit, and each side must balance the other. This rule of balance serves as a built-in risk control, ensuring the counterbalancing effect of every financial transaction.

Debits are recorded on the left side, and credits on the right. Here is a basic example of how accounting transactions appear in a journal entry:

July 5, 20XX		
Office Supplies	$200.00	
Cash		$200.00
To record the purchase of office supplies		

A financial transaction must have left and right sides (debit and credit) that balance. There can be more than one account that makes up the debits or credits. In the example above, there is one row for debits (Office Supplies for $200) and one row for credits (Cash for $200). A transaction can have unlimited rows for each side of the journal entry, as long as the total of all debits equals the total of all credits. In the example below, we see two rows for debits (Office Supplies for $150 and Postage for $50 — total of $200). The credit side has only one row (Cash for $200), but both sides equal the same amount.

July 5, 20XX		
Office Supplies	$150.00	
Postage	$50.00	
Cash		$200.00
To record the purchase of office supplies and postage		

Each line of a transaction is assigned to an account. In the example above, the accounts are Office Supplies, Postage and Cash. Transactions are recorded in account ledgers. An account ledger is a collection of transactions that have been assigned to a particular account. Three ledgers will be affected by the transaction above: Office Supplies, Postage, and Cash. Both Office Supplies and Postage will have a debit entry and Cash will have a credit entry. The tables here are a visual representation. *(Table 1.1)*

TABLES 1.1 — EXAMPLE ACCOUNT LEDGERS

Office Supplies Ledger		
Date	Debit	Credit
7/5/20XX	$150.00	
Subtotal	**$150.00**	

Postage Ledger		
Date	Debit	Credit
7/5/20XX	$50.00	
Subtotal	**$50.00**	

Cash Ledger		
Date	Debit	Credit
7/5/20XX		$200.00
Subtotal		**$200.00**

TABLE 1.1 — MULTIPLE TRANSACTIONS

Cash Ledger/Multiple Transactions		
Date	Debit	Credit
6/25/20XX		$20.00
6/29/20XX		$600.00
7/1/20XX	$400.00	
7/5/20XX	$1,000.00	
7/5/20XX		$200.00
Subtotal	**$580.00**	

Debits - Credits = Subtotal $1,400 - $820 = $580

The next level of data organization is the general ledger. The **general ledger** combines all of the individual account ledgers and is presented in order of the account type. Account types and financial report organization is presented later in this chapter.

Consider the following sequence of events for a distillery:

- On 6/25 spends $20 on office supplies
- On 6/29 spends $600 on tasting room supplies
- On 7/4 receives $400 from tasting room sales
- On 7/5 receives $1,000 from sales to an account who pays cash on delivery
- On 7/5 spends $200 for $150 of office supplies and $50 of postage

TABLE 1.2 — GENERAL LEDGER

Date	Account	Debit	Credit
6/25/20XX	Cash		$20.00
6/29/20XX	Cash		$600.00
7/1/20XX	Cash	$400.00	
7/5/20XX	Cash	$1,000.00	
7/5/20XX	Cash		$200.00
7/4/20XX	Sales: Tasting Room		$400.00
7/5/20XX	Sales: Wholesale		$1,000.00
6/25/20XX	Office Supplies	$20.00	
7/5/20XX	Office Supplies	$150.00	
7/5/20XX	Postage	$50.00	
6/29/20XX	Tasting Room Supplies	$600.00	

The compiled general ledger lists all transactions in order of account type. The general ledger for these events appear in Table 1.2.

Notice in the general ledger that the total of all debits also equals the total of all credits. The presentation of the general ledger does not include a subtotal for debits and credits, but if you added up all amounts in the debit column it will match the sum of amounts in the credit column. In this case, $2,220.

If you remember only one thing from the paragraphs above, remember this: **every accounting transaction must balance.**

Once transactions have been recorded into a company's ledger, the total of each account is presented on a financial report. A full set of financial reports includes the balance sheet, income statement, and statement of cash flows. See chapters two and three for more information on financial reports.

BASIS OF ACCOUNTING

One of the fundamentals for this language of business is the basis on which it is presented. Think of **basis of accounting** as being equivalent to syntax in language. (Syntax is the word order for a language.) There are multiple bases of accounting, but the two most common are *cash basis* and *accrual basis*.

Cash basis accounting recognizes revenue when cash is received and recognizes expenses when cash is disbursed. If goods were sold to a customer today, and the customer pays in 30 days, the revenue would be recognized when cash is received 30 days from today.

Accrual basis recognizes revenue and expenses in the period incurred, regardless of when cash is disbursed or received. Accrual basis employs Accounts Receivable (A/R) and Accounts Payable (A/P), and adheres to GAAP (generally accepted accounting principles). For example, if goods are sold in July, but payment not received until August, a business would increase Accounts Receivable and Sales in July; in August the business would increase Cash and decrease Accounts Receivable.

AUTHOR'S NOTE: Generally accepted accounting principles, commonly referred to as GAAP, is a set of standardized processes that are issued by the Financial Accounting Standards Board (FASB). FASB is a nonprofit organization responsible for setting financial accounting standards for organizations in the United States. GAAP aims to improve the clarity, consistency, and comparability of the communication of financial information.

CHART OF ACCOUNTS

The master list of all accounts is called a chart of accounts. The chart of accounts is further organized into 8 types of accounts:

1. Assets
2. Liabilities
3. Equity
4. Income
5. Cost of Goods Sold
6. Expense
7. Other Income
8. Other Expense

An asset is a resource owned by an entity with an expected future economic benefit. Examples include cash, accounts receivable, inventory, fixed assets (machinery, computers, furniture, equipment, vehicles, etc). Assets can be current or noncurrent. A current asset is an item, such as cash, accounts receivable, and inventory, expected to turn into cash within the next year. A noncurrent asset refers to items that are expected to turn into cash more than a year in the future.

Fixed assets are large purchases of property, plant and equipment that have a useful life of more than one year. Instead of recording the purchase of a fixed asset in the current period, the purchase is capitalized — in other words, recorded on the balance sheet — and expensed over the useful life of the asset. The process of expensing an asset over its useful life is called depreciation.

A liability is an obligation to pay in the future. Examples include accounts payable, loans, or other debt instruments. Like assets, liabilities can be current or noncurrent. A current liability must be paid or settled within a year; noncurrent liabilities will be paid at some point beyond one year from inception. Accounts payable and payroll liabilities are examples of current liabilities; long-term loans are noncurrent liabilities.

Equity represents the value of assets less liabilities. The terminology used for equity will vary depending on a company's structure. Examples of common terminology include retained earnings, partner capital, capital stock, and additional paid-in capital.

There is a relationship between assets, liabilities and equity, and understanding this relationship is key to understanding an analyzing financials. The amount of total assets will always be equal to the sum of total liabilities plus total equity. Viewed as an equation:

Assets = Liabilities + Equity

-or-

Equity = Assets - Liabilities

Assets, liabilities and equity are presented on the balance sheet.

Income is revenue that a company earns from the sale of goods. This could be wholesale revenue, onsite sales revenue, event revenue, merchandise revenue. Any item sold that relates to company operations is income.

Cost of Goods Sold is how much a company spends on an item that it sells to a consumer. Commonly called COGS, Cost of Goods Sold comprises direct materials, direct labor, and manufacturing overhead.

Expenses are other costs not directly associated with items that are sold. For example, the salary for an IT department is an administrative expense not directly tied to the product that a company sells.

Other Income and Expenses are items of income and expense not ordinarily incurred in the normal course of business. For example, if a tank is sold, a gain on that sale would be captured as Other Income because selling a tank is not part of a company's core operations. Therefore, any gain or loss from the transaction will be presented separately from financial accounts related to core operations.

Income, cost of goods sold, expenses, other income and other expense are presented on the Income Statement.

The Income Statement is also commonly called the Profit and Loss Statement; these terms are synonymous.

CHAPTER **TWO**

Balance Sheet and Income Statement

Continuing to build on the analogy of accounting as a language, the "paragraphs" (i.e., ledgers) are compiled and organized to tell a story, like a chapter. These are the financial reports. There are three reports that comprise a full set of financials: balance sheet, income statement, and statement of cash flows. Continuing with the analogy, each full set of financials could be considered a book.

Financial reports communicate to the reader different aspects of the distillery's performance. The balance sheet shows the health of a company at a moment in time. The income statement, or profit and loss statement (P&L) shows the performance of a distillery over a period of time. Income statement and Profit and Loss statement are synonymous terms. The statement of cash flows shows the sources and uses of cash over a period of time.

***AUTHOR'S NOTE:** There are some limitations to a financial statement. The quantitative data on the face of the financials may not answer all of a reader's questions about an organization. For example, the financial information does not speak to the quality of goods produced, nor does it provide information about the efficiency of an organization.*

The statement may lack the detail needed for a business leader to make decisions. For example, information related to product mix of goods sold may not be visible in financial statements. For this reason, many companies prepare their own ancillary reports, such as Margin by SKU, that provide detail necessary to make informational management decisions. Even though standard financial reports may not answer all of a business owner's questions, these standard financial reports are indispensable when measuring the performance of a company.

BALANCE SHEET COMPONENTS

The balance sheet has three major sections: assets, liabilities and equity.

Assets

An asset is a resource owned by an entity with an expected future economic benefit. Assets can be current or noncurrent.

Liabilities

A liability is an obligation to pay in the future. Liabilities can be current or noncurrent.

Equity

Equity represents the amount of money that would be paid to company owners if all assets were liquidated and debts were settled.

Retained earnings is the sum total of all income or loss that a company has earned over time. At the end of each reporting period, the net income (or loss) from the period is closed to the retained earnings account. For example, if retained earnings is $2,000 and the current period's net income is $500, then at the close of the period, the $500 of net income will be added to the existing $2,000, thereby increasing retained earnings to $2,500. At the end of the year when net income closes to retained earnings, the income statement is wiped clean and a new income statement begins.

Assets = Liabilities + Equity. The equation must always be balanced.

The balance sheet *(Table 2.1)* is a summary view. Several of the individual accounts have been collapsed to show a condensed version of the balance sheet. An unconsolidated view of the balance sheet is illustrated in Table 2.2.

TABLE 2.1 Summary View of Balance Sheet

As of December 31, 2019

ASSETS		
Current Assets		
Checking/Savings	188,568.86	CURRENT ASSETS
Accounts Receivable	280,300.96	
Other Current Assets	232,620.57	
Total Current Assets	701,490.39	
Fixed Assets	92,461.47	NONCURRENT ASSETS
Other Assets	380,771.76	
TOTAL ASSETS	**1,174,723.62**	
LIABILITIES & EQUITY		
Liabilities		
Current Liabilitites		
Accounts Payable	195,233.28	CURRENT LIABILITIES
Credit Cards	10,780.15	
Other Current Liabilities	536,722.04	
Total Current Liabilities	742,735.47	
Long Term Liabilities	368,831.27	NONCURRENT LIABILITIES
Total Liabilities	1,111,566.74	
Equity	63,156.88	EQUITY
TOTAL LIABILITIES & EQUITY	**1,174,723.62**	

TABLE 2.2 Unconsolidated View of Balance Sheet

As of December 31, 2019

Item	Amount	Section
ASSETS		Current Assets
Current Assets		Current Assets
Checking/Savings		Current Assets
Cash on Hand	62.24	Current Assets
Checking #1234	187,509.28	Current Assets
Checking #2345	997.34	Current Assets
Total Checking/Saving	188,568.86	Current Assets
Accounts Receivable		Current Assets
Accounts Receivable	280,300.96	Current Assets
Total Accounts Receivable	280,300.96	Current Assets
Other Current Assets		Current Assets
Credit Cards Receivable	22,083.14	Current Assets
Inventory	210,537.43	Current Assets
Total Other Current Assets	232,620.57	Current Assets
Total Current Assets	701,490.39	Current Assets
Fixed Assets		Noncurrent Assets
Accumulated Amortization	-4,678.91	Noncurrent Assets
Accumulated Depreciation	-1,332,506.22	Noncurrent Assets
Artwork	4,850.00	Noncurrent Assets
Computer	3,492.28	Noncurrent Assets
Distillery Equipment	1,159,779.33	Noncurrent Assets
Leasehold Improvments	192,391.21	Noncurrent Assets
Tasting Room Equipment	18,382.78	Noncurrent Assets
Vehicles	50,751.00	Noncurrent Assets
Total Fixed Assets	92,461.47	Noncurrent Assets
Other Assets		Noncurrent Assets
Assets not yet in service	374,221.76	Noncurrent Assets
Rent Deposit	6,550.00	Noncurrent Assets
Total other assets	380,771.76	Noncurrent Assets
TOTAL ASSETS	**1,174,723.62**	Noncurrent Assets

Item	Amount	Section
LIABILITIES & EQUITY		Current Liabilities
Liabilities		Current Liabilities
Current Liabilitites		Current Liabilities
Accounts Payable		Current Liabilities
Accounts Payable	195,233.28	Current Liabilities
Total Accounts Payable	195,233.28	Current Liabilities
Credit Cards		Current Liabilities
Credit Card	9,715.24	Current Liabilities
First Bank CC #3456	664.91	Current Liabilities
First Bank CC #4567	400.00	Current Liabilities
Total Credit Cards	10,780.15	Current Liabilities
Other Current Liabilities		Current Liabilities
Gift Card Liability	2,215.34	Current Liabilities
Keg Deposits Received	41,386.95	Current Liabilities
Line of Credit	478,354.75	Current Liabilities
Pallet Deposits	2.432.00	Current Liabilities
Payroll Liabilities	10,585.80	Current Liabilities
Tips Payable	1,747.20	Current Liabilities
Total Current Other Liabilities	536,722.04	Current Liabilities
Total Current Liabilities	742,735.47	Current Liabilities
Long Term Liabilities		Noncurrent Liabilities
First Bank #6789	235,389.38	Noncurrent Liabilities
First Bank #5678	69,701.89	Noncurrent Liabilities
Loans Payable	63,740.00	Noncurrent Liabilities
Total Long Term Liabilities	368,831.27	Noncurrent Liabilities
Total Liabilities	1,111,566.74	Noncurrent Liabilities
Equity		Equity
Members Equity	-122,464.46	Equity
Retained Earnings	185,621.34	Equity
Total Equity	63,156.88	Equity
TOTAL LIABILITIES & EQUITY	**1,174,723.62**	

BALANCE SHEET ANALYSIS

The balance sheet reveals the health of a distillery. While the income statement provides important information about sales and profitability, it can mask other financial problems. If a distillery has incurred too much debt, for example, or if there is not enough cash available to continue operations for the short term, a reader will not see this on the income statement, but they will on the balance sheet.

***AUTHOR'S NOTE** In my opinion, the most useful way to read a balance sheet is by watching the period-over-period changes in account groups. The change over time is more useful than the face value of the current period's report.*

As a operator, seeing that long term liabilities have decreased $100,000 from one period to another is probably more helpful than seeing that the current balance of long term liabilities is $900,000. Without historical context, the current balance has less meaning.

The interpretation of a company's health from the balance sheet lies in measuring the movement of account values over time, and the relationship between different accounts on the balance sheet. The face value of an account provides very little helpful information without the horizontal and vertical context: that is, the context in respect to prior periods (horizontal) as well as an account's relationship to others on the balance sheet (vertical). For example, a steady decline in Accounts Receivable for three months in a row is a signal that some or all of the following could be occurring:

1. the distillery has entered a slow season;
2. sales are dropping; or
3. there could be cash flow problems in the future.

The context in which a monthly balance sheet is presented is key to extracting meaning from the report. Horizontal and vertical analysis is covered in Chapter Four — Interpreting Financial Statements.

INCOME STATEMENT

The income statement has four primary sections:

- Revenue
- Cost of goods sold
- Expenses
- Other Income/Expenses

Revenue shows how much was sold. Cost of Goods Sold shows how much was spent to produce the items sold, Expenses are other operating expenses of the company, and Other Income/Expenses are amounts earned or spent not related to day-to-day operations. An income statement will always follow the same order: revenue followed by COGS followed by Expenses followed by Other Income/Expenses. The specific accounts displayed on the income statement will not always be the same; those entries will depend on the specific company's chart of accounts.

The income statement reflects a company's performance over a period of time. *(Sample appears in Table 2.3).*

COST OF GOODS SOLD

It's more important than ever to understand the business of spirits. Market forces are causing disruption and increased competition leading to more choices for the consumer. This tighter environment results in a price ceiling of what the consumer is willing to pay. At the same time, suppliers are largely limited to the same shelf space with more brands. The more competitive environment coupled with distributor consolidation, fickle consumers, and challenging access to retailers means that producers must understand the margin of each product they produce.

Margin is the difference between revenue and cost of goods sold; therefore, to understand margin a producer needs to understand what goes into COGS.

TABLE 2.3 Sample Income Statement

	TOTAL	
Ordinary Income/Expense		
Income		
Discount	-22,450.49	Revenue
Food Sales	321,605.38	
Merchandise Sales	11,340.00	
N/A Beverage Sales	9,020.75	
Sales of Product Income	60.00	
Spirits Sales	1,092,939.92	
Wine Sales	8,095.50	
Total Income	1,420,611.06	
Cost of Goods Sold		
Excise Tax	18,600.72	Cost of Goods
Food COGS	102,452.15	
Gas/Oxygen	10,347.66	
Merchandise COGS	7,467.98	
N/A Beverage COGS	1,142.00	
Shipping & Delivery	6,253.50	
Spirits COGS	499,441.19	
Wine COGS	2,971.79	
Total COGS	648,676.99	
Gross Profit	771,934.07	
Expense		
Amortization	333.99	Expenses
Bank Service Charges	1,285.55	
Charitable Contributions	1,362.27	
Computer and Internet Expenses	1,238.99	
Depreciation Expense	16,332.24	
Dishwasher Service	1,968.48	
Dues and Subscriptions	632.68	
Employee Benefits	15,487.57	
Gift Cards	39.57	
Gifts	817.59	
Guaranteed Payment	24,000.00	
Insurance Expense	12,137.15	Expenses
Interest Expense	12,187.56	
Janitorial Expense	3,921.70	
Lab Supplies	5,721.04	
Landscaping	533.88	
Licenses & Permits	393.70	
Marketing	13,455.61	
Meals	286.00	
Merchant Fees	10,747.00	
Office Supplies	4,443.82	
Payroll	75,345.29	
Payroll Service Fee	2,283.60	
Postage and Delivery	9,061.98	
Professional Fees	22,101.18	
Rent Expense	46,211.92	
Repairs and Maintenance	20,710.62	
Sales Expense	18,262.74	
Small Wares	2,525.95	
Supplies	25,834.28	
Tasting Room Labor	301,251.45	
Taxes	2,819.00	
Telephone/Cable/Internet	2,986.44	
Utilities	32,077.89	
Total Expense	688,798.73	
Net Ordinary Income	83,135.34	
Other Income/Expense		
Other Income		
Gain/Loss on Sale of Equipment	15,000.00	Other Income Expenses
Other Income	1,000.00	
Total Other Income	16,000.00	
Net Other Income	16,000.00	
Net Income	99,135.34	

The following should be included: *(Table 2.4)*

- Raw Materials
- Barrels
- Production labor
- Excise tax
- Manufacturing overhead
- Depreciation

Table 2.4

Expense Type	Classify as COGS
MATERIALS	
Raw Materials	Yes
Packaging Materials	Yes
Freight in	Yes
Associated Taxes on Goods Purchased	Yes
LABOR (wages, taxes, benefits)	
Distillers and cellarmen	Yes
Packaging	Yes
Maintenance/engineering	Yes
Warehouse	Yes
Director of operations	Yes
Lab and Quality Control	Yes
Sales and Marketing	No
IT and HR	No
Tasting Room	No
Administrative	No
Officer	No
OVERHEAD	
Rent	Yes
Utilities	Yes
Excise Tax	Yes
Insurance (product-related)	Yes
Waste (dumped product)	Yes
Vendor returns	Yes
Depreciation on production equipment	Yes
Memberships and Subscrip-tions	Yes
Consumables, service and parts	Yes
Production repairs and maintenance	Yes
Pallets	Yes

The purchase of raw materials is an asset. They move through the production process and stay an asset until the finished good is sold. Direct labor and a portion of overhead are also allocated to the cost of inventory. The stages of inventory are unfinished inventory, work in process (WIP), and finished goods.

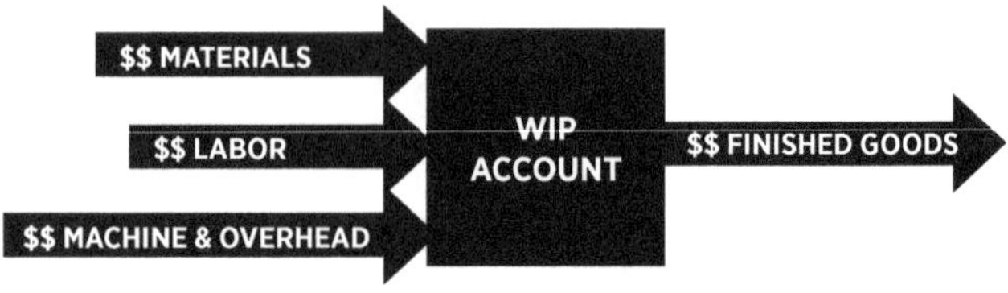

WORK IN PROCESS	
Debit	**Credit**
Work In Process (WIP)	Raw Materials
	Applied Overhead

The chart above shows the financial effect of the first step of the production process. When the production process begins, raw materials become WIP. Raw materials decrease (credit) and WIP increases (debit). Balances move from one inventory account to another. Everything stays on the balance sheet. Nothing has moved to the income statement.

FINISHED GOODS	
Debit	**Credit**
Finished Goods	WIP
	Packaging Materials

Above, we see the next step of the production process: moving from WIP to Finished Goods. Again, balances move from one inventory account to another. Everything stays on the balance sheet. Nothing has moved to the income statement.

COST OF GOODS SOLD	
Debit	**Credit**
Cost of Goods Sold	Finished Goods

Finally, a finished good is sold. Costs are recognized only when an item is sold. Balances move from the balance sheet to the income statement.

AUTHOR'S NOTE **HOW TO BREAK OUT LABOR AND OVERHEAD RELATED TO PRODUCTION**

If you are like many small businesses, your payroll and overhead may be reported in the operating expense portion of your income statement. How do you separate the portion of labor and overhead related to COGS and include it in the correct section of the balance sheet? First, let's consider how most small businesses process and record payroll. Payroll for the entire company will be recorded on the books as Payroll Expense in the operating section — a debit to Payroll Expense and a credit to Cash.

Payroll Expense	$10,000	
Cash		$10,000
To record January 31 payroll		

To record COGS payroll, first create departments in your payroll reports. Logistically, this can be achieved by assigning each employee to a department. Your payroll reports will then provide departmental totals, and the expense will be booked accordingly. Let's assume that total payroll of $10,000 comprises $6,000 production labor, $2,000 administrative labor, and $2,000 sales labor. With a payroll report by department, the entry would look like this:

COGS — Production Labor	$6,000	
Administrative Labor	$2,000	
Sales Labor	$2,000	
Cash		$10,000
To record January 31 payroll		

A more advanced option for recording COGS payroll is to build the standard payroll cost per unit produced into the bill of materials (BOM) for the item you are producing. For example, if your standard cost of labor to produce a case of vodka is $2.00, that standard payroll amount would be built into the BOM for that item. This method requires using a clearing account to adjust for any difference between the standard labor cost and the actual labor cost. See chapter five for a detailed description.

Labor is only one component of overhead that can be attributed to COGS. Other overhead items include manufacturing overhead (utilities, rent, etc.), depreciation related to production equipment, and excise tax. To record other overhead items correctly, a similar practice is followed. A company will derive a standard cost of overhead related to each good produced. This cost, say, $3.00, will be built into the BOM of each item produced. A clearing account will be used to adjust for any difference between the standard overhead allocated versus the actual overhead used in production.

One of the simplest and most helpful ways to analyze costs is by understanding the break-even point. This is the point at which a company has sold enough product that costs are covered. With each successive sale net income is generated. The break-even point can be calculated in dollars or units.

In order for break-even to be calculated correctly, all costs in an organization must be classified as either fixed or variable. Fixed costs do not change over a relevant range; rent is an example of a fixed cost. Rent will be the same if one case is produced, or if ten thousand cases are produced; however, in terms of cost per unit, fixed costs decrease per unit as more units are produced. Variable costs behave in the opposite way. The total cost of a variable expense — for example, raw ingredients — will increase as the number of cases produced increases; however, in terms of cost per unit, variable costs stay the same, regardless of how many cases are produced.

AUTHOR'S NOTE ***To classify a cost as either fixed or variable is applicable only within a relevant range. Over the long term, all costs are variable. Every cost will increase as an operation grows. Take rent, for example. A production facility can manufacture only X number of units. Once the facility reaches capacity, a larger facility will be required, which in turn raises costs.***

Beak-Even Units

Fixed costs / (Sales price per unit — Variable costs per unit)

Break-Even Sales

Fixed costs / Contribution Margin per unit *(Table 2.5)*

Table 2.5

	Total	Per Unit
Sales (1,000 units)	$100,000	$100
Less: Variable Costs	($60,000)	($60)
Contribution Margin	$40,000	$40
Less: Fixed Costs	($30,000)	($30)
Net Income	$10,000	$10
Contribution Margin Ratio		40%
Break-even revenue		$75,000
Break-even units		750

To include a target profitability, say, $50,000, that figure must be built into the equation as if it were a fixed cost:

Break-even revenue: ($30,000 + $50,000)/40% = $200,000. Break-even units: $200,000/$100 per unit = 2,000 units.

This calculation demonstrates that, with the current cost structure, to make $50,000 in profit, this company must sell 2,000 units.

Knowing break-even point is helpful, but if a company is selling multiple products that each have their own profitability, more analysis is needed. To take it to the next level, consider the product mix of a company. This mix could be as simple as spirit type, or as complex as a SKU-level break even analysis. *Knowing the break-even point for a company's specific sales mix can truly drive actionable data.*

***AUTHOR'S NOTE** Assume a company sells three products: vodka, gin, whiskey. Each product is only sold in one pack type (e.g., a case of 750mL bottles). The contribution margin of the products is 55%, 50%, and 40%, respectively. Assume fixed costs for the distillery is $320,000. Using this information, you can determine the break-even units per brand.*

With this calculation you can optimize the target sales mix to achieve break-even. *(Table 2.6)*

Table 2.6

	Vodka	Gin	Whiskey
Fixed costs	$320,000	$320,000	$320,000
Contribution margin	55%	50%	40%
Break-even revenue	$581,818	$640,000	$800,000
Sales price per case	$145	$150	$220
Break-even units	4,013	4,267	3,636

EBITDA

In the Income Statement example shown earlier in this chapter, EBITDA is absent as a line item. EBITDA is a common metric used to evaluate the performance of a company, but it is not a specific line item in an income statement. Rather, it is calculated from multiple parts of the income statement. You will not see EBITDA in a traditional income statement in GAAP format.

EBITDA stands for Earnings Before Interest Taxes Depreciation and Amortization.

EBITDA = Net Income + Interest + Taxes + Depreciation + Amortization

Generally speaking, EBITDA of 5% is unsustainably low, 10% is good, and 15% is very good.

***AUTHOR'S NOTE** EBITDA is commonly used to judge the performance of a company because it levels the playing field, so to speak, for financial differences that may arise due to differences in the structure of companies.*

For example, consider Distiller A who incurred $1 million of bank debt to begin operations. This entity will pay interest to the bank as it pays back the loan. The income statement for Distiller A will include — let's say — $50,000 of interest expense per year. Now compare that to Distiller B who is funded by a wealthy founder. In all other respects Distiller B is exactly like Distiller A. Because Distiller B has no bank debt, the company will also not have the $50,000 of interest expense dragging down net income. Without consideration of this difference, Distiller A would appear to be a much more poorly managed operation than Distiller B. But that's not the case! They are, in fact, equally well-run organizations. This is just one example of how EBITDA accounts for differences in company structure and gives stakeholders a way to view multiple companies, apples to apples.

Financial benchmarks should be different for each line of business. A line of business is a way of organizing activity in a company. For example, if a company produces both beer and spirits, the company would consider each type of beverage a separate line of business, although a producer could also think of sales channels as lines of business, such as wholesale sales and retail sales.

When financial data is being organized, each line of business or sales channel should be separated via Classes or Departments. (See chapter five for a detailed discussion of this topic.) Well-organized financials allow management to compare the performance of different business lines to the correct industry benchmarks. One of the most common areas for improvement in distillery financials is in tasting room COGS.

Many distilleries assign the same cost to tasting room sales of spirits as they do to the cost of wholesale sales. Tasting room sales should be recorded at arm's length pricing, meaning that the tasting room recognizes COGS as if the spirit inventory were purchased from an unaffiliated third party. When product made in the distillery is sold in the tasting room, the product is effectively sold from one department to another: production distillery sells to the tasting room; tasting room purchases from the production facility. Management should review performance of each department separately and judge each on its own merits.

When an arm's-length price is charged for the goods sold in a tasting room, each line of business's profitability is calculated. Granted, the relationship between a production facility and tasting room is symbiotic, and both serve the same master — the investors but to measure the economic reality of each division's performance, it is critical that the production distillery get 'credit' for the sale of goods to the tasting room, and that the tasting room be burdened with a true arm's-length price for COGS. Although it may seem that this practice will lead to double counted revenue and COGS, this is resolved by booking an intracompany elimination entry.

To implement arm's-length pricing, the double-counted revenue (i.e., the sale of the spirits from the production facility to the tasting room) must be backed out through a contra-revenue account (if using vertical analysis), or through a revenue account tagged as Administrative (if using horizontal analysis). Similarly, the double-counted COGS (that is, the purchase of spirits by the tasting room) must be backed out through a contra-COGS account or through a COGS account tagged as Administrative.

Consider Distillery XYZ. The distillery has a

production facility that sells spirits to wholesale accounts and has a restaurant that offers a full menu. The company is profitable, but management feels that the brewpub is underperforming, although they can't identify why. Without data on performance by line of business, they will not know that the pub is losing money and is overstaffed. Therefore, they cannot hold the pub general manager accountable. The Controller implements classes so that management can see the performance of the pub. They distillery begins selling beer to the restaurant at an arm's-length price, which results in a more realistic representation of that division's profitability. The result is that areas of weakness are identified, and clear instruction is given to the general manager. The company leadership now knows what needs to be adjusted.

***AUTHOR'S NOTE** I strongly recommend using arm's-length pricing so that management can clearly see the performance of each segment of a company. Here are two examples of how this revenue might appear in a monthly income statement:*

Example A *(Table 2.7)*

You see that the administrative class has a negative revenue and equal amount of negative COGS. This balances the intracompany sales and therefore the Total column is correctly stated. Each class gets proper credit for its sales without compromising the integrity of the financials.

Table 2.7

DISTILLERY ABC / PROFIT AND LOSS
JAN-18

	Administrative	Tasting Room	Wholesale	TOTAL
Ordinary Income/Expense				
Income				
Discounts	0.00	-5,466.13	-700.50	-6,166.63
Food Sales	0.00	82,745.25	0.00	82,745.25
Merchandise Sales	0.00	1,337.50	0.00	1,337.50
Miscellaneous	0.00	0.00	0.00	0.00
N/A Beverage Sales	0.00	1,699.25	0.00	1,699.25
Room Rental	0.00	0.00	0.00	0.00
Spirits Sales	-21,194.97	52,995.02	113,000.38	144,800.43
Wine Sales	0.00	2,728.00	0.00	2,728.00
Total Income	-21,194.97	136,038.89	112,299.88	227,143.80
Cost of Goods Sold				
Excise Tax	0.00	0.00	9,381.72	9,381.72
Food COGS	0.00	25,765.08	0.00	25,765.08
Gas/Oxygen	0.00	325.00	762.08	1,087.08
Keg Expense	0.00	0.00	1,830.00	1,830.00
Merchandise COGS	0.00	810.77	0.00	810.77
N/A Beverage COGS	0.00	421.50	0.00	421.50
Shipping & Delivery	0.00	0.00	2,484.00	2,484.00
Spirits COGS	-21,194.97	43,368.97	15,331.29	37,505.29
Wine COGS	0.00	1,056.63	0.00	1,056.63
Total COGS	-21,194.97	71,747.95	29,789.09	80,342.07
Gross Profit	0.00	64,290.94	82,510.79	146,801.73

Example B *(Table 2.8)*

In this example, the distillery separates each business line by vertical divisions. Intracompany Sales/COGS serves as the contra-account, which wash the double-counted revenue and COGS.

Table 2.8

DISTILLERY EFG / PROFIT AND LOSS APR-18	
	Total
Income	
Restaurant Sales	742,169.60
Brewery Sales	358,099.51
Distillery Sales	53,436.57
Intracompany Sales	-122,631.23
Total Income	**$1,031,074.45**
Cost of Goods Sold	
Restaurant COGS	447,069.14
Brewery COGS	260,645.12
Distillery COGS	32,735.28
Intracompany COGS	-122,631.23
Total Cost of Goods Sold	**$617,818.31**
Gross Profit	**$413,256.14**

CHAPTER **THREE**

Statement of Cash Flow

Managing cash is a critical skill and a topic that affects companies of all industries, ages, and sizes. Two tools are relevant for cash flow management: a cash flow statement and a cash flow forecast. A cash flow *statement* shows the sources and uses of cash over a period of time, while a cash flow *forecast* looks to the future.

The **statement of cash flows** is the link between the balance sheet and the income statement. It shows readers the sources and uses of cash. It can be structured in the direct method or the indirect method. The indirect method is most commonly used; it begins with net income and accounts for period-over-period changes on the balance sheet.

There are three main sections on the Statement of Cash Flows:

- Operating Activities
- Investing Activities
- Financing Activities

The operating activities section includes movement of cash from your core operations. The net cash flow from operations answers the question "How much cash was generated from operations over the period?

The cash flow from investing section accounts for changes in cash related to investing activities. A common activity in the investing section is buying or selling fixed assets. This section also includes changes in accumulated amortization and depreciation. The net cash provided by investing activities answers the question "How much cash was generated from investments over the period?"

Cash flow from financing accounts for changes in cash related to the receipt of debt proceeds or

Table 3. 1

DISTILLERY ABC / STATEMENT OF CASH FLOWS

	Jan - Dec 18	
OPERATING ACTIVITIES		
Net Income	99,135.34	Cash Flow from Operations
Adjustments to reconcile Net Income to net cash provided by operations:		
Accounts Receivable	-117,182.86	
Credit Cards Receivable	-8,300.01	
Inventory:Finished Goods:Cases Packaged	-69,784.14	
Inventory:Finished Goods:Kegs	-6,705.13	
Inventory:Merchandise	-4,808.18	
Inventory:Packaging Materials	64,990.39	
Inventory:Raw Materials	52,875.39	
Inventory:Tasting Room Inventory:Food	-925.30	
Inventory:Tasting Room Inventory:Guest Spirits	35.21	
Inventory:Tasting Room Inventory:N/A Beverages	30.00	
Inventory:Tasting Room Inventory:Spirits	27.02	
Inventory:Tasting Room Inventory:Wine	153.75	
Inventory:Work in Process	-4,058.33	
Accounts Payable	-80,346.74	
First Bank CC #3456	3.28	
First Bank CC #4567	-879.00	
Gift Card Liability	-3,394.83	
Keg Deposits Received	-7,410.00	
Line of Credit	-23,501.21	
Payroll Liabilities	-30,046.46	
Tips Payable	-270.00	
Net cash provided by Operating Activities	-140,361.81	
INVESTING ACTIVITIES		
Accumulated Amortization	333.99	Cash Flow from Investing
Accumulated Depreciation	-5,801.76	
Distillery Equipment	-3,372.80	
Leasehold Improvements	-3,755.43	
Tasting Room Equipment	-1,093.00	
Assets Not Yet In Service	-21,429.76	
Net cash provided by Investing Activities	-35,118.76	
FINANCING ACTIVITIES		
First Bank #6789	-11,060.62	Cash Flow from Financing
Frist Bank #5678	-20,061.51	
Net cash provided by Financing Activities	-31,122.13	
Net cash increase for period	-206,602.70	
Cash at beginning of period	395,171.56	
Cash at end of period	188,568.86	

repayment of debt, or is related to receipt of cash injections from or distributions to investors. It answers the question "How much cash was generated from financing activities over the period?" *(Table 3.1)*

Tables 3.2a, b and c show how the income statement and balance sheet feed into the statement of cash flows. Notes have been added to explain how certain figures were calculated.

When a distillery uses financial reports to analyze performance, company leaders must understand the difference between cash flow and profitability. Cash flow is the change in cash within a period. Profitability is tied to accrual accounting and reflects to the economic reality of a business, regardless of cash effects.

Table 3.2a

INCOME STATEMENT
YEAR ENDING 12/31/2021

Revenue	100,000
(COGS)	-50,000
Gross Margin	50,000
(Operating Expenses)	-36,000
(Depreciation Expense)	-5,000
(Interest Expense)	-4,000
Net Income	**5,000**

Table 3.2b

BALANCE SHEET

	12/31/2021	12/31/2020	$ Change
Cash	205,000	190,000	15,000
Accounts Receiveable	50,000	40,000	10,000
Inventory	10,000	12,000	-2,000
Fixed Assets	405,000	370,000	35,000
(Accumulated Depreciation)	-130,000	-125,000	-5,000
Total Assets	**40,000**	**487,000**	**53,000**
Accounts Payable	35,000	43,000	-8,000
Notes Payable	368,000	360,000	8,000
Total Liabilities	403,000	403,000	0
Equity	137,000	84,000	53,000
Total Liabilities & Equity	**540,000**	**487,000**	**53,000**

$53,000 includes $5,000 from current year income and $48,000 of equity contributions.

Table 3.2c

STATEMENT OF CASH FLOWS
YEAR ENDING 12/31/2021

Net Income	5,000
Depreciation Expense	5,000
Change in A/R	-10,000
Change in Inventory	2,000
Changes in A/P	-8,000
Cash from Operating Activities	**-6,000**
Change in Fixed Assets	-35,000
Cash from Investing Activities	**-35,000**
Change in Notes Payable	8,000
Change in Equity	48,000
Cash from Financing Activities	**56,000**
Net Change in cash	15,000
Beginning of period cash	190,000
End of period cash	**205,000**

Table 3.3 illustrates the difference. Assume a company issues five invoices per month at $2,000 per invoice. Payment terms are net 21. COGS are 50% of revenue and operating expenses are $3,000 per month.

The monthly net income line represents profitability, while the monthly cash flow line represents cash flow. Note: While the company has been profitable both months, it is still not cash flow positive by the end of Month 2.

Table 3.3

	Month 1	Month 2
Issued invoice	5	5
Value per invoice	$2,000	$2,000
Paid invoices	0	5
Booked revenue	$10,000	$10,000
Cash received	$0	$10,000
COGS	$5,000	$5,000
Operational costs	$3,000	$3,000
Monthly net income	$2,000	$2,000
Monthly cash flow	($8,000)	$2,000
Cumulative cash flow	($8,000)	($6,000)

***AUTHOR'S NOTE:** This illustration highlights the difference between net income — profitability — and cash flow. To focus only on profitability would be foolish because a company can easily run out of cash and still be profitable.*

Cash is king. It's the life blood of any business. Often, cash flow is more important to manage than profitability, especially when a company is in start-up or growth mode. A company with positive cash flow has increasing liquid assets, which means that the company can pay down debt, reinvest in business, return profits to shareholders, and provide a financial buffer for lean times.

The health of a company's cash position is measured by liquidity ratios and efficiency ratios. (See Ch. 8 for more info.) The cash conversion cycle has a major impact on a company's cash position. Simply stated, the cash conversion cycle is the amount of time between spending a dollar on an expense to the point where the dollar appears as profit on sales. In the spirits industry, where so much cash is tied up in inventory, not to mention the long inventory maturation cycle, having strategies to shorten cash conversion cycle is critical. A strong cash conversion cycle will allow the producer to fund growth with internally generated cash, as opposed to borrowing cash and paying interest.

AUTHOR'S NOTE: IDEAS FOR SHORTENING THE CASH CONVERSION CYCLE:

Consider tightening up AR and AP days to add days — or months — of cash on hand to the bottom of your cash flow statement. Negotiate shorter payment terms for customers on account. Some distributors will agree to Net 20 payment terms.

Consider selling club memberships or taking preorders of releases. This will generate more predictable cash flow and will allow you to take in cash before inventory is delivered.

If selling to a distributor or state liquor agency, arrange for electronic payment whenever possible. This will minimize undue lag time of mail delivery and subsequent deposit of a check.

Using a credit card for business expenses is a good strategy as long as the balance is paid off in a timely manner and little interest is incurred. Using a credit card reduces the cash conversion cycle by 30 days. Buying raw materials today with a credit card postpones the cash hit of that expense for another month. Credit cards are a great cash flow tool when used properly. But they can also be a slippery slope. Bottom line: Proceed with caution!

Of course, the ultimate strategy for improving cash flow is to improve gross margin. Don't forget to negotiate with your suppliers. One distillery shared this anecdote: they invited five suppliers, including the current supplier, to bid on its contract for 750mL clear bottles. The suppliers in the bid had been vetted to include only those who could provide a bottle of comparable quality to their current one. The distillery previously paid $39 per carton of glass, and the winning bid came in at $37. This savings per bottle now adds an additional $12,000 to the bottom line and reduces the cash conversion cycle.

Real-Life Application

BENDISTILLERY

I joined Bendistillery about twenty years ago in 2000. Jim our founder had just started the company a few years before. It was a fairly new concept at the time; we were one of the first craft distilleries in the country. He and I had been friends for several years and I was looking for a new opportunity at the time, so it was a risk. I came in doing sales, then that turned into doing all of the marketing and events. About seven years ago, Jim stepped away a little bit and I became the CEO of the company, and we have grown since then. I had no prior experience in distilling or the liquor industry, except for a stint bartending at the Deschutes Brewery in my early days. My skill set grew as the industry grew. I don't think you could do what I did if you were starting today. I hit the industry at the right time. Since I began, the industry has matured and competition has grown to the point that much more refined skill sets are needed today to do what really was a bootstrapped operation twenty years ago.

The traditional advertising and marketing tools weren't available to us at Bendistillery when I began because we really didn't have the budget for it. We had to quickly embrace much more grassroots marketing efforts any way we could. We were very much an event-oriented company. Our marketing company was going out and sampling drinks...winning people over one person at a time.

When I joined in 2000 I think there couldn't have been more than twenty craft distilleries in the US. It was a really small field of producers, so as we looked for guidance we looked at the beer and wine industries, and in other aspects we figured it out as we went along. I think that was not because beer was a great model for us, but because Bend had such a well-developed craft beer community. Beer producers were really the only people available to us who seemed to know what they were doing. As it turned out, the consumer expectations and marketing details ended up being quite a bit different for spirits than they are for beer. We ended up having to change things considerably down the road because we had built ourselves kind of on a craft beer model, but the way that people buy spirits is much different than how they buy beer.

I would say that on the event side the wine industry was a better model to follow because there were a lot of small wine producers. We definitely watched them and took a page out of their playbook. But we really made a lot of this up as we went along.

Since our backyard was Oregon, Washington, and Idaho — all of which were control states when we began — it was a very simple distribution model. You just asked the state for a listing and your product was then available statewide. It was then up to us to develop the consumer pull. We used brokerages almost immediately to help us out with the on-premise sales. We moved into the open state distribution model — first in California — pretty quickly. Never to much success. Certainly, more success back then than we have now. Distributors have very much controlled access to the market. That's gotten worse as there's been more and more consolidation in the industry. The ability to get into the direct-to-consumer sales channel is something that has really started to develop in the last year, and is a very small portion of our business, but is definitely growing.

We use fulfillment companies for direct-to-consumer sales. From the consumer side, the whole model appears to be DTC, but it really is following the three tier system. We are still dealing with a company who buys from the distributor through a licensed retailer in a state and ships out from there, so it's still very much predicated on states that allow shipments of spirits into their market. From that perspective it hasn't changed that much. We're still using the same model, but a new tool of that model, to ship to consumers. Coupled with social media it has opened up really efficient ways to reach the end consumer and I think it is going to dramatically change the industry over the next few years. I think distributors still view on-premise as their domain and have used their size and clout, particularly coming out of the pandemic, to roadblock all but their biggest brands. So, it's setting up this two tier retail system. If you are seeking out something other than a big brand, it's going to be at an off-premise package store or through some online channel, whereas bars and restaurants are still serving the same seven or eight brands you've always seen. And beer has done that too. You might see eighteen or twenty tap handles, but somehow half or more are all owned by the same company. The catalyst for change will be consumer demand. Eventually I think it will overwhelm distributor resistance, or laws will change which will disrupt the distribution model. I think that middle tier will somehow open up and put some competition back into the industry.

As CEO, I am looking at our general ledger almost every day. What I'm looking for varies quite a bit, depending on what's on my mind at the moment. I'm looking at the P&L twice a month; I'm looking at the budget once a week; I'm looking at individual product line profitability quite frequently because the marketing people are always asking if we can run discounts or this or that SKU, or we are thinking about a new product release. I have a very attentive CFO who manages everything from bookkeeping to the larger financial picture and she's very cash flow oriented because she and her team are actually writing the checks, so she looks at bank accounts multiple times a day.

I'd say to any upcoming distillery: pay more attention to cash flow than anything else, because it is such a huge deal for our company. We never have terms longer than net 30 with our suppliers, and our distributors might pay us at 45 or 60 days. If we're dealing with a control state, even if we are shipping pallets, we only get paid on bottles sold. If you are in any sort of growth phase, cash is the biggest problem you'll have.

Because of the nature of our industry, it is really difficult to accelerate inflows and decelerate outflows. At any given time we need two to three months of cash for operations. Especially when you are growing to the point to take advantage of economies of scale. We are beyond that point fortunately, so I don't have to worry about getting my best price on packaging materials, but that wasn't always the case.

We were a classic entrepreneurial company. Our founder did everything, and bookkeeping was one of the last things he gave up because he wanted to keep tabs on cash. If you are an entrepreneur immediately identify what your skill set is; if you aren't a bookkeeper, hire one. That doesn't mean that you can't write the checks or keep a focus on cash, but you don't need to do the data entry. That should be an early hire. Whether that is a CFO or Controller really depends on who you have working for you. We have about thirty-five employees and we still are organized more on the skill set of the people who have been with us a long time as opposed to the perfect org chart you'd design if doing it from scratch. Its' a case-by-case basis for assigning responsibilities to the skills within the company. Occasionally we get lucky and a good person walks in the door and we find a position for them that fills an open spot within the company, but I think we are probably a year or so away from reorganizing in a way that would make a business professor happy.

We were profitable from day one and that had a lot to do with timing. We were founded in the days of gin and vodka. The production cycle of products was seven days. Now whiskey is the most popular spirit and there's a lot of capital sunk into the product before you make money on it. I can't imagine trying to start a distillery today and trying to play in the space where everyone wants to be now.

I'm fortunate our business is in the position it is, and cash flow management has a lot to do with it. It's one of those things that's so obvious to people that sometimes it just doesn't get the attention that it needs.

Alan Dietrich is the CEO of Bendistillery in Bend, Oregon

CASH FLOW FORECASTING

Cash flow is the lifeblood of a business, and cash flow management can be particularly tricky for a distillery. Spirits have significant overhead in products, and many products age in barrels for several years while producers must continue to pay rent and utilities each month during the aging process.

The strain on cash flow is magnified when a distiller brings a new spirit to market. There are significant amounts of time, effort, and hard costs to launch a new product. Those expenses will be incurred well before they generate revenue.

The best tools for managing cash in a distillery are a cash flow forecast, a safety net of cash, and sufficient access to credit. As the liquor industry becomes more competitive, it is important to tighten the core of business. A strong business core will allow a producer to operate nimbly, react quickly, go further and faster, and be more resilient.

A cash flow forecast is a management tool that identifies projected low points of cash and aids in strategic planning.

AUTHOR'S NOTE: I recommend using a thirteen-week cash flow forecast that is updated weekly. After the first thirteen weeks, I recommend building a forecast by month for the second quarter and by quarter for the remainder of the year.

The biggest benefit of cash flow forecasting is becoming aware of low points in cash before they are upon you. Forecasting allows the management to source funds proactively before lack of cash becomes an urgent situation. With a weekly projection, a manager can fine-tune bill payments when cash is tight. Moving one large bill payment by just a few days might be what's needed to keep a positive cash balance. Cash flow forecasting provides a detailed view of the coming quarter's cash position so that managers can reduce surprises. Forecasting also gives managers a stronger understanding of the distillery's annual business cycle.

Table 3.4 is an example of a cash flow forecast document. Built in Excel, there are multiple tabs. The first is a summary tab that gives an overview of

Table 3.4

	A	B	C	D	E	F	G	H	I	J	K	L	M	N	O	P	Q
2	Distillery ABC																
3	CF Forecast Summary																
4	12.31.19																
5																	
6			**Week Starting**														
7			**12/29/2019**	**1/5/2020**	**1/12/2020**	**1/19/2020**	**1/26/2020**	**2/2/2020**	**2/9/2020**	**2/16/2020**	**2/23/2020**	**3/1/2020**	**3/8/2020**	**3/15/2020**	**3/22/2020**		
8	Receipt of AR		$ -	$ 155,372	$ -	$ 44,816	$ 56,049	$ 179,888	$ -	$ 88,725	$ -	$ 95,000	$ -	$ 102,000	$ -		
9	Payment of AP		$ (3,927)	$ 5,054	$ 4,637	$ 6,789	$ 72	$ -	$ -	$ -	$ -	$ -	$ -	$ -	$ -		
10	OpEx detail		$ (28,500)	$ (6,500)	$(105,500)	$ (6,500)	$ (70,500)	$ (24,603)	$ (53,082)	$ (18,022)	$ (62,500)	$ (32,603)	$ (59,836)	$ (18,022)	$ (62,500)		
11	Investing and Financing		$ (8,267)	$ -	$ -	$ 25,000	$ (8,267)	$ (30,000)	$ -	$ -	$ (8,267)	$ -	$ -	$ -	$(150,000)		
12	Change in cash		$ (40,694)	$ 153,926	$(100,863)	$ 70,104	$ (22,646)	$ 125,285	$ (53,082)	$ 70,703	$ (70,767)	$ 62,397	$ (59,836)	$ 83,978	$(212,500)		
13																	
14	Beginning cash		$ 502,350	$ 461,656	$ 615,582	$ 514,719	$ 584,823	$ 562,177	$ 687,462	$ 634,379	$ 705,082	$ 634,315	$ 696,712	$ 636,876	$ 720,854		
15	Ending cash		**$ 461,656**	**$ 615,582**	**$ 514,719**	**$ 584,823**	**$ 562,177**	**$ 687,462**	**$ 634,379**	**$ 705,082**	**$ 634,315**	**$ 696,712**	**$ 636,876**	**$ 720,854**	**$ 508,354**		
16																	
17	Margin of safety		$ (500,000)	$(500,000)	$(500,000)	$(500,000)	$(500,000)	$(500,000)	$(500,000)	$(500,000)	$(500,000)	$(500,000)	$(500,000)	$(500,000)	$(500,000)		
18	Available cash		**$ (38,344)**	**$ 115,582**	**$ 14,719**	**$ 84,823**	**$ 62,177**	**$ 187,462**	**$ 134,379**	**$ 205,082**	**$ 134,315**	**$ 196,712**	**$ 136,876**	**$ 220,854**	**$ 8,354**		
19																	
20																	
21																	
22																	
23																	
24																	
25																	
26																	
27																	
28																	
29																	
30																	
31																	
32																	

SUMMARY | AR Aging Detail | AP Aging Detail | OpEx Detail | Investing and Financing Detail | Historical Income Statement | Income Statement Pivot

cash position. Following the summary are tabs for accounts receivable, accounts payable, operating expenses, investing and financing, a historical income statement, a pivot table of the income statement, and others as needed.

The summary tab aggregates data from all of the individual tabs and presents it in one spot. It displays on a weekly basis the projected change in cash, beginning and ending cash balance, margin of safety, and available cash.

Margin of safety is the cash on hand. I recommend keeping at least three months of cash burn on hand. Consider cash burn to be everything except direct materials and hourly production labor. Margin of safety is the resources available to a company if production were to halt and you needed to pay bare bones expenses for a period of time. Average monthly cash burn is determined by using the following calculation with data from the last twelve months:

(Total COGS + Total Operating Expenses — Direct Materials — Hourly Production Labor — Depreciation — Amortization) / 12 = Average monthly burn

Once the margin of safety is deducted from the ending cash balance, the available cash represents the amount of discretionary cash that is projected to be on hand.

Each subsequent tab feeds into the Summary tab. With this structure, a manager can fine-tune the bills to be paid on any given week and have a hawk's eye to cash flow. This forecasting tool is a must-have for navigating a volatile environment that changes daily. The last thing any manager wants is to be caught off-guard with a shortage of cash.

The AR tab lists individual receivables in rows. (*Table 3.5*) The open amount should be assigned to the weekly column during which the company expects to receive the cash. The receivables in the Accounts Receivable balance only account for sales that have already been invoiced, and cash in this account is expected to be collected within a few weeks. But because the forecast is built to accommodate thirteen weeks into the future, a manager must decide how to account for the sales expected to occur later in the quarter and which are not yet on the books as AR invoices. This can be resolved by adding two other

Table 3.5

Row		Date	Num	Customer	Due Date	Past Du	Open Amount
2	AR Aging Detail						
3	12.31.19						
4							
5		Date	Num	Customer	Due Date	Past Du	Open Amount
6	1 - 30 days past due						
7		11/10/2019	1867	Distributor A	12/10/2019	21	43,844.17
8		11/10/2019	1872	Distributor B	12/10/2019	21	152.11
9		11/16/2019	1886	Distributor A	12/16/2019	15	58,244.92
10	Total for 1 - 30 days past due						$ 102,241.20
11	Current						
12		12/11/2019	1901	Distributor A	1/10/2020	-10	56,048.80
13		12/11/2019	1902	Distributor B	1/10/2020	-10	53,130.40
14		12/23/2019	1903	Distributor A	1/22/2020	-22	69,116.10
15		12/23/2019	1904	Distributor B	1/22/2020	-22	44,815.72
16		12/23/2019	1905	Distributor A	1/22/2020	-22	65,851.80
17	Total for Current						$ 288,962.82
18	Subtotal						$ 391,204.02
19							
20	Sales Orders						
21		Date	Num	Customer	Proj. Due Date		Proj. Amount
22		12/20/2019	SO823	Distributor A	2/5/2020		38,725.00
23		12/20/2019	SO824	Distributor B	2/5/2020		44,920.00
24							83,645.00
25	Forecasted Sales Orders						
26		Date	Num	Customer	Proj. Due Date		Projected Amount
27		1/15/2020		Distributor A	2/20/2020		45,000.00
28		1/15/2020		Distributor B	2/20/2020		50,000.00
29		1/31/2020		Distributor A	3/5/2020		52,000.00
30		1/31/2020		Distributor B	3/5/2020		50,000.00
31		2/15/2020		Distributor A	3/20/2020		55,000.00
32		2/15/2020		Distributor B	3/20/2020		50,000.00
33							302,000.00
34							
35	TOTAL						$ 776,849.02
36							
37							
38							
39							
40							
41							

Row	Week Starting 12/29/2019	1/5/2020	1/12/2020	1/19/2020	1/26/2020	2/2/2020	2/9/2020	2/16/2020	2/23/2020	3/1/2020	3/8/2020	3/15/2020	3/22/2020	TC
7		$ 43,844.17												
8		$ 152.11												
9		$ 58,244.92												
12					$ 56,048.80									
13		$ 53,130.40												
14						$ 69,116.10								
15				$ 44,815.72										
16						$ 65,851.80								
18	$ -	$ 155,371.60	$ -	$ 44,815.72	$ 56,048.80	$ 134,967.90	$ -	$ -	$ -	$ -	$ -	$ -	$ -	$
22	$ -	$ -	$ -	$ -	$ -	$ -	$ -	$ 38,725	$ -	$ -	$ -	$ -	$ -	
23	$ -	$ -	$ -	$ -	$ -	$ 44,920	$ -	$ -	$ -	$ -	$ -	$ -	$ -	
24	$ -	$ -	$ -	$ -	$ -	$ 44,920	$ -	$ 38,725	$ -	$ -	$ -	$ -	$ -	$
27	$ -	$ -	$ -	$ -	$ -	$ -	$ -	$ -	$ -	$ 45,000	$ -	$ -	$ -	
28	$ -	$ -	$ -	$ -	$ -	$ -	$ -	$ 50,000	$ -	$ -	$ -	$ -	$ -	
29	$ -	$ -	$ -	$ -	$ -	$ -	$ -	$ -	$ -	$ -	$ -	$ 52,000	$ -	
30	$ -	$ -	$ -	$ -	$ -	$ -	$ -	$ -	$ -	$ 50,000	$ -	$ -	$ -	
31	$ -	$ -	$ -	$ -	$ -	$ -	$ -	$ -	$ -	$ -	$ -	$ -	$ -	
32	$ -	$ -	$ -	$ -	$ -	$ -	$ -	$ -	$ -	$ -	$ -	$ 50,000	$ -	
33	$ -	$ -	$ -	$ -	$ -	$ -	$ -	$ 50,000	$ -	$ 95,000	$ -	$ 102,000	$ -	$
35	$ -	$ 155,372	$ -	$ 44,816	$ 56,049	$ 179,888	$ -	$ 88,725	$ -	$ 95,000	$ -	$ 102,000	$ -	$

SUMMARY | AR Aging Detail | AP Aging Detail | OpEx Detail | Investing and Financing Detail | Historical Income Statement | Income Statement Pivot

Ready

sections to the AR tab: sales orders and projected sales orders. The data in the sales orders section represent sales orders received from customers but not yet shipped. The data in the forecasted sales orders section represents the orders expected to be received, but which have not yet occurred. This allows the manager to track the amount of anticipated revenue over the entire future thirteen week period.

Likewise, on the AP tab, *(Table 3.6)* individual vendor bills (payables) are listed in rows and the payment is assigned to the column that corresponds to the date when the payment will be made. Note that this is not simply the bill's due date; this should reflect when a company will write a check and thus the timing should account for days in transit to the vendor. Assume bills will be paid 7 days before the due date — this allows time for transit if a check is delivered by mail.

Listing each individual AP invoice gives managers greater flexibility to arrange payments in a very detailed fashion, which is extremely helpful if cash is tight.

Note that the AP Aging Detail tab includes only costs that are already on the books as AP invoices. Generally, these costs will take us out four weeks into the future. A company will not have bills due in week 13 in its accounting file because those expenses have not yet been incurred. Where do we account for those future expenses that are not yet in AP? On the operating expenses tab.

Table 3.6

	A	B	C	D	E	F	G	I	J	K	L	M	N	O	P	Q	R	S	T	U	V
1	Distillery ABC																				
2	AP Aging Detail																				
3	12.31.19																				
4								Week Starting													
5		Date	Num	Vendor	Due Da	Past D	Amou	12/29/2019	1/5/2020	1/12/2020	1/19/2020	1/26/2020	2/2/2020	2/9/2020	2/16/2020	2/23/2020	3/1/2020	3/8/2020	3/15/2020	3/22/2020	TOTAL
10		12/19/2019	29465	Service Provider C	12/19/2019	53	32.00		32.00												
11		12/20/2019	122019	Utility B	12/20/2019	52	1,428.58	1,428.58													
12		12/24/2019	2481074	Service Provider A	12/24/2019	48	52.11		52.11												
13		11/25/2019	9574	Contract Canning	12/25/2019	47	5,032.12				5,032.12										
14		11/25/2019	10994	Raw Material C	12/25/2019	47	186.53			186.53											
15		11/26/2019	2019281	Raw Material B	12/26/2019	46	940.00	940.00													
16		12/26/2019	122619	Utility A	12/26/2019	46	227.75	227.75													
17		11/30/2019	119151	Service Provider C	12/30/2019	42	275.81			275.81											
18		12/10/2019	116166	Raw Material A	12/30/2019	42	1,656.16	1,655.16													
19	Total for 1 - 30 days past due						$ 11,971.26	5,095.66	1,381.14	462.34	5,032.12	-	-	-	-	-	-	-	-	-	
20	Current																				
21		12/11/2019	117058	Raw Material A	12/31/2019	41	1,648.80	1,648.80	-	-	-	-	-	-	-						
22		12/11/2019	11291	Raw Material C	12/31/2019	41	1,313.40	1,313.40	-	-	-	-	-	-	-						
23		12/31/2019	2019377	Raw Material B	12/31/2019	41	9,116.10	9,116.10	-	-	-	-	-	-	-						
24		12/31/2019	11894	Raw Material C	12/31/2019	41	-7,815.72	(7,815.72)	-	-	-	-	-	-	-						
25		12/31/2019	1277	ABC Brewery	12/31/2019	41	-15,851.80	(15,851.80)	-	-	-	-	-	-	-						
26		12/02/2019	10835	Service Provider C	01/01/2020	40	62.50	62.50	-	-	-	-	-	-	-						
27		12/13/2019	INV-0118054	Raw Material A	01/02/2020	39	287.10	287.10	-	-	-	-	-	-	-						
28		12/18/2019	121819	Utility A	01/02/2020	39	648.36	648.36	-	-	-	-	-	-	-						
29		12/19/2019	901356	Serice Provider B	01/03/2020	38	211.95	211.95	-	-	-	-	-	-	-						
30		12/05/2019	11056	Raw Material C	01/04/2020	37	1,357.06	1,357.06	-	-	-	-	-	-	-						
31		12/17/2019	118762	Raw Material A	01/06/2020	35	1,665.32	-	1,665.32	-	-	-	-	-	-						
32		12/19/2019	180024	Raw Material D	01/08/2020	33	1,379.20	-	1,379.20	-	-	-	-	-	-						
33		12/19/2019	120265	Raw Material A	01/08/2020	33	81.40	-	81.40	-	-	-	-	-	-						
34		12/11/2019	11082	Raw Material C	01/10/2020	31	546.95	-	546.95	-	-	-	-	-	-						
35		12/16/2019	10905	Service Provider C	01/15/2020	26	62.50	-	-	62.50	-	-	-	-	-						
36		12/31/2019	1633	Bookkeeper	01/15/2020	26	665.00	-	-	665.00	-	-	-	-	-						
37		12/31/2019	123119	Accounting Firm	01/15/2020	26	400.00	-	-	400.00	-	-	-	-	-						
38		12/18/2019	9661	Contract Canning	01/17/2020	24	3,046.85	-	-	3,046.85	-	-	-	-	-						
39		12/30/2019	122702	Raw Material A	01/19/2020	22	845.90	-	-	-	845.90	-	-	-	-						
40		12/31/2019	123370	Raw Material A	01/20/2020	21	709.00	-	-	-	709.00	-	-	-	-						
41		12/31/2019	521919	Utility C	01/20/2020	21	201.56	-	-	-	201.56	-	-	-	-						
42		12/31/2019	119354	Service Provider C	01/30/2020	11	72.15	-	-	-	-	72.15	-	-	-						
43	Total for Current						$ 653.58	(9,022.25)	3,672.87	4,174.35	1,756.46	72.15	-	-	-						
44	Subtotal						$ 12,624.84	(3,926.59)	5,054.01	4,636.69	6,788.58	72.15	-	-	-	-	-	-	-	-	12,624.84

SUMMARY | AR Aging Detail | AP Aging Detail | OpEx Detail | Investing and Financing Detail | Historical Income Statement | Income Statement Pivot

The operating expenses tab includes recurring expenses such as payroll that do not come in the form of a bill, and future operating expenses for which the bill has not yet been received. *(Table 3.7)*

The top section, *Expenses — generally not invoiced*, includes predictable monthly expenses plus "Other," which is a placeholder for the average weekly unplanned expenses. The bottom section, *Expenses — generally invoiced*, includes those expenses for which a company expects to receive a bill. Note that the first four to five weeks will be grayed out with no data in the cells. This is because any AP that will be due in that timeframe has already been received as a vendor bill, and thus is included on the AP Aging Detail tab.

The tabs Historical Income Statement and Income Statement Pivot are reference tabs. The historical income statement tab shows the income statement by month for the last 24 months. A company in business less than 24 months should include as many months' data as possible. To the left of the data, an added column assigns one of the major expense categories from the OpEx Detail tab. In this case, the options are:

- Guaranteed Payments
- Payroll
- Rent
- Taxes
- Other
- Direct Materials
- Insurance
- Maintenance
- Professional Fees
- Supplies
- Utilities

Table 3.8 is an excerpt from the historical income statement tab, and it shows the major expense category assignment in the first column, followed by the specific

Table 3.7

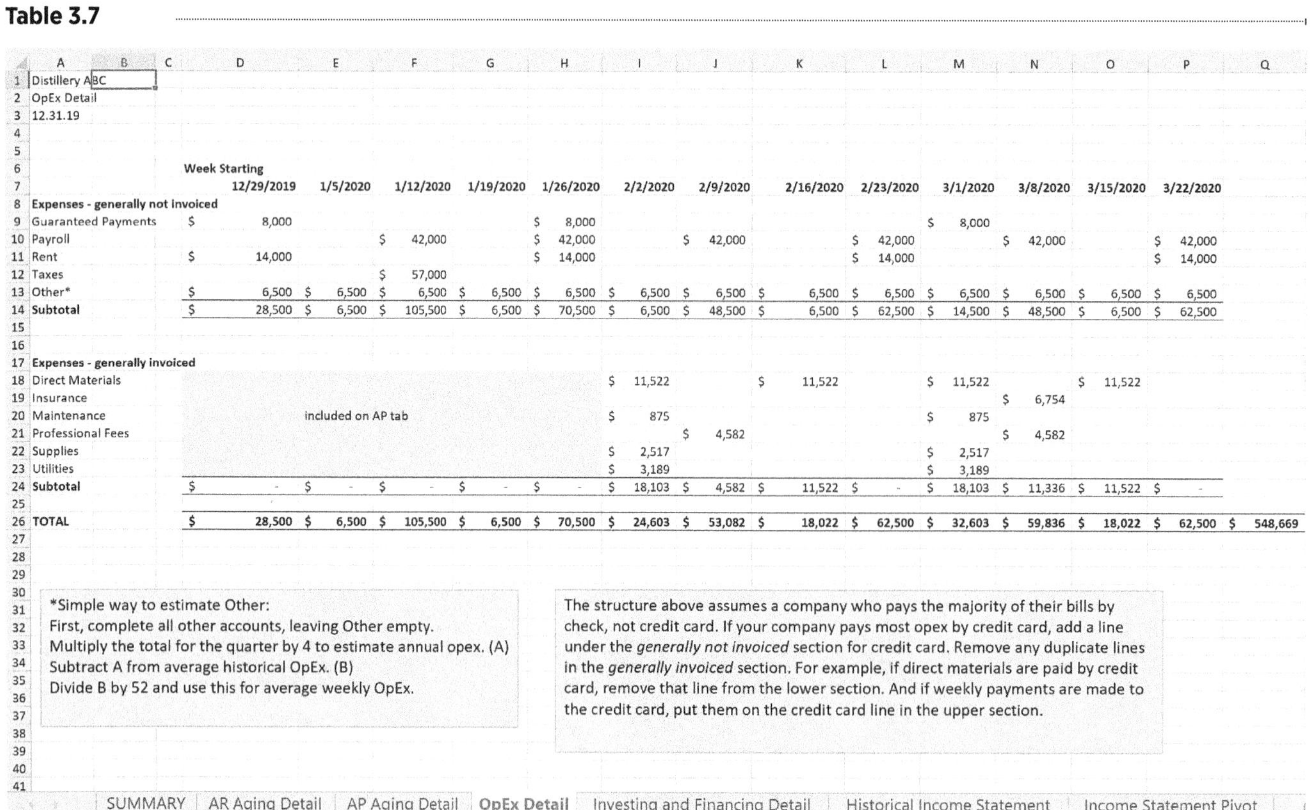

Distillery ABC
OpEx Detail
12.31.19

Week Starting	12/29/2019	1/5/2020	1/12/2020	1/19/2020	1/26/2020	2/2/2020	2/9/2020	2/16/2020	2/23/2020	3/1/2020	3/8/2020	3/15/2020	3/22/2020	
Expenses - generally not invoiced														
Guaranteed Payments	$ 8,000				$ 8,000					$ 8,000				
Payroll			$ 42,000		$ 42,000		$ 42,000		$ 42,000		$ 42,000		$ 42,000	
Rent	$ 14,000				$ 14,000				$ 14,000				$ 14,000	
Taxes			$ 57,000											
Other*	$ 6,500	$ 6,500	$ 6,500	$ 6,500	$ 6,500	$ 6,500	$ 6,500	$ 6,500	$ 6,500	$ 6,500	$ 6,500	$ 6,500	$ 6,500	
Subtotal	$ 28,500	$ 6,500	$ 105,500	$ 6,500	$ 70,500	$ 6,500	$ 48,500	$ 6,500	$ 62,500	$ 14,500	$ 48,500	$ 6,500	$ 62,500	
Expenses - generally invoiced														
Direct Materials						$ 11,522		$ 11,522		$ 11,522		$ 11,522		
Insurance											$ 6,754			
Maintenance			included on AP tab			$ 875				$ 875				
Professional Fees							$ 4,582				$ 4,582			
Supplies						$ 2,517				$ 2,517				
Utilities						$ 3,189				$ 3,189				
Subtotal	$ -	$ -	$ -	$ -	$ -	$ 18,103	$ 4,582	$ 11,522	$ -	$ 18,103	$ 11,336	$ 11,522	$ -	
TOTAL	$ 28,500	$ 6,500	$ 105,500	$ 6,500	$ 70,500	$ 24,603	$ 53,082	$ 18,022	$ 62,500	$ 32,603	$ 59,836	$ 18,022	$ 62,500	$ 548,669

*Simple way to estimate Other:
First, complete all other accounts, leaving Other empty.
Multiply the total for the quarter by 4 to estimate annual opex. (A)
Subtract A from average historical OpEx. (B)
Divide B by 52 and use this for average weekly OpEx.

The structure above assumes a company who pays the majority of their bills by check, not credit card. If your company pays most opex by credit card, add a line under the *generally not invoiced* section for credit card. Remove any duplicate lines in the *generally invoiced* section. For example, if direct materials are paid by credit card, remove that line from the lower section. And if weekly payments are made to the credit card, put them on the credit card line in the upper section.

SUMMARY | AR Aging Detail | AP Aging Detail | **OpEx Detail** | Investing and Financing Detail | Historical Income Statement | Income Statement Pivot

account in the second column, and the monthly results for that account in the following columns.

Table 3.8

Supplies	6009 Small Equipment		510.70	847.57
Misc	6010 Shipping & delivery expense	188.27	265.00	154.38
Maintenance	6011 Repair & Maintenance	168.10	55.00	1,898.11
Supplies	6012 Lab Expense			
Supplies	6013 Keg Expense	206.36	125.00	

The next tab, Income Statement Pivot, will be a pivot table of the data in the Historical Income Statement tab. The rows of the pivot table will include the major expense categories. *(Table 3.9)*

This pivot table will be used on the OpEx tab. For example, if a company pays insurance quarterly, the week that includes the payment date will have a formula that references the sums of the months for which a payment is being made. A payment made on December 15 to cover insurance for January, February and March will reference the average annual sum of the insurance line's January, February and March columns on the income statement pivot.

The cash flow forecasting workbook takes a lot of time to build and requires effort to maintain, but the payoff is a valuable tool that can be used daily to guide a business through the tight cash situations that inevitably will arise.

CASH FLOW BEFORE PROFITABILITY

In the early years of a company, managing cash flow should be of greater importance than managing profitability. Manufacturers often are tempted to buy ingredients or packaging materials in large quantities to take advantage of price discounts. A company should avoid buying in bulk if it means inventory will be sitting on the warehouse floor for longer than approximately three months. (Of course, logistics and availability of needed materials must be considered. Also, there are clear exceptions for product that is aging in barrels.) Buying solely on unit price and

Table 3.9

DISTILLERY ABC
HISTORICAL INCOME STATEMENT PIVOT TABLE
12.31.19

Row Labels	Sum of Jan 2018	Sum of Feb 2018	Sum of Mar 2018	Sum of Dec 2019	Sum of Total
Amortization					1,037.00
Debt Service	1,968.28	1,870.16	1,791.84	2,396.94	46,306.88
Depreciation					1,054.44
Direct materials	11,211.70	15,030.37	12,401.27	13,122.00	536,961.71
Excise Tax	2,449.93	659.00	641.02	128.00	18,038.00
Guaranteed Payments	7,000.00	7,000.00	7,000.00	12,500.00	174,080.00
Insurance	1,318.00	1,044.15	1,308.00	843.00	26,228.74
				1,778.41	20,378.35

ignoring the cash effect of large purchases is one of the most common mistakes that entrepreneurs make when it comes to managing cash.

Optimal inventory level should be pegged to the future months' COGS. The sales forecast can give a distillery the information needed to determine the optimal amount of ingredients and packaging to buy each month. Achieving lean production in a distillery is, admittedly, a lofty goal, but just being aware of the impact of the production cycle on available cash will help a manager move towards lean manufacturing.

As a company grows, a brand may receive large purchase orders that are unexpected and which cause a cash crunch. (The distillery must spend money on inputs or labor to fulfill the order, and these needs can stress the organization). Small businesses often finance these unexpected peaks of sales with a line of credit. Once the company matures and has a rhythm of sales established, it becomes easier to build working capital from profits of the operation and a line of credit can become less of a requirement.

CHAPTER **FOUR**

Interpreting Financial Statements

The Chart of Accounts is the list of all accounts in a company's general ledger. Every chart of accounts, regardless of company or industry, will have a similar structure, but the individual accounts will be specific to each company based on its unique needs and preferences. Over the years in which I've worked with beverage alcohol companies I have never encountered the same chart of accounts twice.

ORGANIZING THE CHART OF ACCOUNTS

Designing a chart of accounts requires a balance of detail versus summary. It may seem advantageous to create an account for every specific type of expense, but this can lead to unwieldy reports that become very difficult to read. At the same time, too few accounts does not provide enough information to take action. The goal is to have enough information but not too much.

***AUTHOR'S NOTE:** A sample chart of accounts is included in the Appendix. Use this as a starting point as you build your chart of accounts. Refine it and make it your own.*

A manager must begin with the end in mind. Primary considerations are the audience who will be using the data, and how it will be used. For example, if there are multiple revenue centers, then leadership may want to view each separately. Imagine setting a chart of accounts for a distillery who sells wholesale, and also has onsite sales where drinks are served over the counter and bottles are purchased by patrons for off-premise consumption. It is important that reports are structured so that the performance of each business center *and* the performance of the company as a whole can be viewed. There are two ways to design the chart of accounts to achieve that visibility: the use of classes for horizontal analysis or the use of divisions for vertical analysis.

Classes are a way of organizing data into groups. In the example above, the classes would be Wholesale, Tasting Room, and Administrative. Each transaction in a company's accounting records would be tagged with a Class so that when reports are viewed, each Class would appear as a separate column. Because we are looking across the page at different departments, we call this horizontal analysis. Classes give a manager the flexibility to run reports with separate columns visible, or without separation for a holistic view of the company.

In the excerpt below, the revenue section of this income statement shows four columns: administrative, tasting room, wholesale, and total. The administrative class has no revenue associated with it because it is a cost center. The tasting room class shows revenue from the company's retail location, and the wholesale class is sales to the state liquor control agency. With classes, Distillery ABC sees how each sales channel is performing on its own, and how the company is performing as a whole. *(Table 4.1)*

Classes are an option in several accounting software programs like Quickbooks. When recording a sale, the class field is used to tag the transaction so that it shows up in the correct column. In the invoice below, each row is tagged with Tasting Room class, which

Table 4.1

DISTILLERY ABC / PROFIT & LOSS BY CLASS
JANUARY - DECEMBER 2018

	Administrative	Tasting Room	Wholesale	TOTAL
Ordinary Income/Expense				
Income				
Discounts	0.00	-22,450.49	0.00	-22,450.49
Food Sales	0.00	321,605.38	0.00	321,605.38
Merchandise Sales	0.00	11,214.00	126.00	11,340.00
N/A Beverage Sales	0.00	9,020.75	0.00	9,020.75
Spirits Sales				
Vodka	0.00	11,210.50	700,880.82	712,091.32
Spirits Sales - Other	0.00	211,092.14	169,756.46	380,848.60
Total Spirits Sales	0.00	222,302.64	870,637.28	1,092,939.92
Wine Sales	0.00	8,095.50	0.00	8,095.50
Total Income	0.00	549,787.78	870,763.28	1,420,551.06

Figure 4.1

Invoice

DATE 01/17/2018

INVOICE # 869

BILL TO

SHIP TO

P.O. NUMBER	TERMS	REP	SHIP	VIA	F.O.B.
	Net 30		01/17/2018		

QUANTITY	ITEM CODE	DESCRIPTION	PRICE EACH	CLASS	AMOUNT
1	Shirts:Men's T-shirts	mens classic shirts	7.00	Taproom	7.00
2	Shirts:Men's T-shirts	new logo shirts	14.00	Taproom	28.00
2	Shirts:Women's T-shirts	womens classic shirts	9.00	Taproom	18.00
1	Hats:Trucker	trucker hats	5.00	Taproom	5.00

assigns the revenue to the Tasting Room. If this were an invoice to a wholesaler, the class would be marked as Wholesale. *(Figure 4.1)*

Another method of analyzing performance is by vertical analysis. Using the same scenario of a distillery that wishes to track wholesale sales and tasting room sales, a report might look like Table 4.2.

Table 4.2

DISTILLERY ABC / PROFIT & LOSS BY CLASS
JANUARY - DECEMBER 2018

		Total
Income		
40000 Restaurant Sales		
40100 Food		
40110 Food Sales		621,614.96
40120 Food Discounts	-$	31,825.02
Total 40100 Food	$	589,789.94
40300 Beverage Sales		
40310 Spirits Sales		173,112.49
40320 Tasting Flights		114,954.26
40340 Wine Sales		50,690.50
Total 40300 Beverage Sales	**$**	**338,757.25**
40400 Merchandise Sales	$	89,052.09
Total 40000 Restaurant Sales	**$**	**1,191,145.84**
43000 Distillery Sales		
43100 Wholesale		
43120 Wholesale Vodka		16,679.27
43140 Wholesale Gin		13,880.08
43160 Wholesale Tequila		10,312.28
43180 Wholesale Whiskey		16,975.40
Total 43100 Wholesale	**$**	**57,847.03**
43300 Retail Liquor Sales		
43320 Retail Vodka		17,669.77
43340 Retail Gin		14,792.16
43360 Retail Tequila		13,317.42
43380 Retail Whiskey		19,597.20
Total 43300 Retail Liquor Sales	**$**	**65,376.55**
Total 43000 Distillery Sales	**$**	**123,223.58**
Total Income	**$**	**1,314,369.42**

In this example there are actually three areas of sales tracked: (1) restaurant sales, which includes sales of spirits served for on-premise consumption; (2) wholesale sales, which includes sales to the state liquor control agency for off-premise sales; and (3) retail sales, which includes sales directly to the consumer for off-premise consumption. Within the Wholesale and Retail sections, there are subaccounts for Vodka, Gin, Tequila and Whiskey. This section is followed by a Retail section with the same structure. This structure still provides enough separation for management to analyze the performance of each sales channel individually, and the performance of the company as a whole.

A distillery using vertical analysis will have a larger chart of accounts than would a company using horizontal analysis. Horizontal analysis allows for a second dimension to the data (Classes). The user can get the same information with fewer accounts. Both methods are acceptable.

Management preference strongly influences the chart of accounts design. Comparing the revenue section of the chart of accounts under each method, the horizontal method allows a revenue section with only 4 accounts. The vertical method results in a revenue section of 9 accounts. Either method works fine, and whatever is chosen must support the goals of management and how that team wants to use the data.

Table 4.3a

COMPARISON OF REVENUE SECTION OF CHART OF ACCOUNTS — HORIZONTAL VS VERTICAL METHODOLOGY

Horizontal (use of Classes)	Vertical (use of Divisions)
Vodka Sales	Wholesale Sales
Gin Sales	Wholesale Sales: Vodka Sales
Tequila Sales	Wholesale Sales: Gin Sales
Whiskey Sales	Wholesale Sales: Tequila Sales
	Wholesale Sales: Whiskey Sales
	Retail Sales
	Retail Sales: Vodka Sales
	Retail Sales: Gin Sales
	Retail Sales: Tequila Sales
	Retail Sales: Whiskey Sales

Whatever method is chosen for setting revenue accounts, the COGS section should mirror the revenue accounts as much as possible. If using the revenue accounts pictured above, the COGS section would include the following accounts:

Table 4.3b

COMPARISON OF COGS SECTION OF CHART OF ACCOUNTS — HORIZONTAL VS VERTICAL METHODOLOGY

Horizontal (use of Classes)	Vertical (use of Divisions)
Vodka COGS	Wholesale COGS
Gin COGS	Wholesale COGS: Vodka COGS
Tequila COGS	Wholesale COGS: Gin COGS
Whiskey COGS	Wholesale COGS: Tequila COGS
	Wholesale COGS: Whiskey COGS
	Retail COGS
	Retail COGS: Vodka COGS
	Retail COGS: Gin COGS
	Retail COGS: Tequila COGS
	Retail COGS: Whiskey COGS

Another common use of classes is to designate geographic areas. If a distillery sells product across the western United States, classes may be organized by region (Pacific Northwest, California/Hawaii, Mountain Central, Southwest), or each state may be designated as a separate class.

Note that the chosen method depends on personal preference and the capabilities of your software to organize data. Not all financial reporting software has the classes functionality.

These types of reports can be easily created from most accounting or POS software.

Another management request may be to increase visibility into different lines of product. Perhaps a distillery offers a well product, a premium product, and also a super-premium product. Certainly, the leadership team will want to see the performance of each line and its associated margins. Again, this is a situation where detail from a Sales by Item report could be pulled. Or if organization by tier seems the most important aspect of a distiller's product mix, then perhaps the revenue and COGS accounts would be organized as in Table 4.4.

Table 4.4

Sales
Well Sales
Premium Sales
Super-premium Sales
Total Sales

COGS
Well COGS
Premium COGS
Super-premium COGS
Total COGS

Under the structure noted above, a company would rely on other reports from the accounting system to show the breakout of type of spirit (vodka, gin, etc) under each tier.

Table 4.5

DISTILLERY EFG / SALES BY ITEM
JANUARY - MARCH, 2018

	Quantity	Total Amount	% of Sales	Avg Price
375 ML GIN	108.00	9,052.96	7%	$ 83.82
750 ML GIN	106.00	39,754.32	32%	$ 375.04
375 ML VODKA	108.00	9,939.79	8%	$ 92.04
750 ML VODKA	160.00	24,040.38	20%	$ 150.25
375 ML TEQUILA	110.00	10,822.99	9%	$ 98.39
750 ML TEQUILA	20.00	3,599.40	3%	$ 179.98
375 ML WHISKEY	9.00	1,799.77	1%	$ 199.97
750 ML WHISKEY	103.00	24,115.02	20%	$ 234.13
Total	724.00	$ 123,124.63		

***AUTHOR'S NOTE** Let's say the chart of accounts is organized in a way that best balances simplicity with adequate detail. In the monthly financial review meeting your sales director asks to add additional accounts. He says that he needs to see the performance on a granular level, and requests to add new accounts for sales of cases of 375mL vs 750mL. In his opinion, the accounts in the chart of accounts don't offer enough detail. Good news! There is a way to provide the requested info without impacting the chart of accounts. Consider pulling a Sales by Item report. This will provide the detail that the sales director seeks, without having to change the chart of accounts. (Table 4.5)*

In chapter two we discussed what should be included in COGS, such as labor and a portion of overhead. But how does a company include something like labor in, say, Gin COGS? There are multiple options, and the best approach depends on the internal resources of a distillery's accounting department and the sophistication and knowledge of those using the financial reports.

Let's zoom in on one of these items of overhead: payroll. There are a few ways to book payroll. The simple approach is to record a debit to payroll expense (an operating expense, not a cost of goods), and a credit to cash. A more complex option is to record payroll by department. In practice, the process looks like this: after payroll is processed, the company receives a report showing the total cost of each department. This might include production labor, tasting room labor and administrative labor. The company could record that expense as follows:

Production Labor (COGS)	$4000	
Tasting Room Labor (OpEx)	$2,500	
Administrative Labor (OpEx)	$1,500	
Cash		$8,000

This journal entry allows the company to allocate correctly some of its labor as COGS.

An advanced option is to include labor in the bill of materials for goods produced. That is, for every unit produced, the cost of that unit will include the raw ingredients cost as well as the bottle's portion of labor and other overhead items. The cost of a bottle of vodka in inventory will include some labor cost. In practice, adding labor cost is complex because a company has already spent the money on payroll, yet this method capitalizes a portion of labor into the inventory. When payroll is capitalized, it will not be expensed until the good is sold. How does a distiller avoid counting payroll twice? To achieve accuracy, the cost of labor must be built into a bill of material by using a standard cost. The journal entry looks something like this:

Inventory Finished Goods Vodka	$500	
Payroll Clearing		$500

The payroll clearing account is a balance sheet account that is used to accumulate payroll costs that are captured in inventory. When regular payroll costs are incurred, they are booked in this same payroll clearing account:

Payroll Clearing	$500	
Cash		$500

The result is that the company doesn't recognize the production payroll as an expense until the goods attached to the payroll are sold. This method is correct under GAAP and provides an economically accurate picture of an organization. However, it is a complex process and may be too complex for some small businesses to implement.

***AUTHOR'S NOTE** This is an example of choosing an accounting method that meets your company's needs and structure. Remember to weigh the costs and benefits of your accounting methodologies. You may find that you spend more time trying to get detailed costs correct, which pushes out the delivery of monthly financials. If the accounting processes are so complex that they slow down the month-end close, then management is provided outdated financials. It's difficult to take action from old information. My recommendation is for small distillers to book payroll expense by department so that it is easy to separate out production payroll from administrative payroll, sales payroll, and tasting room payroll. Production payroll should be included as a separate account in COGS. Only consider building labor and other overhead into the bill of materials when the company becomes more sophisticated with a strong internal accounting team. In my experience, this is the best balance of simplicity and usefulness for a small company.*

If production payroll and other overhead items are separately stated within COGS, then the COGS section of a chart of accounts might look like Table 4.6.

The COGS section doesn't exactly match the revenue section — there are additional accounts (Payroll, Rent and Utilities, etc) — but the direct materials COGS accounts *do* mirror the revenue accounts.

The same process used for payroll overhead can be applied to other overhead items, like rent or utilities expenses. A portion belongs in COGS and a portion belongs in operating expenses. I recommend allocating the expense ratably by % of square footage. Assuming a production area accounts for one third of the total facility, here is the journal entry to record rent:

Rent-Production Facility	$1,000	
Rent-Admin	$2,000	
Cash		$3,000

***AUTHOR'S NOTE** Key takeaway: keep the chart of accounts as simple as is practicable. Remember that you can get details from other sources. It's common for a distillery to use a POS software for onsite sales, like Square or Toast. Also, many producers generate wholesale invoices out of the inventory management system. Each of these programs can generate reports that give detail about what was sold. Remember that you can keep your accounting records high-level and turn to additional software for details about what was sold. Decide which factor leads your decision-making and let the primary factor dictate the organization of revenue accounts.*

In the same spirit, if you use an inventory management software that is separate from your accounting software, do not replicate the build assemblies for items in the accounting software. Duplicating build assemblies in two software programs creates a scenario where you are essentially running parallel systems. It creates more work than is needed. Allow the production process to be documented in the inventory management system and let the accounting software provide the financial results. You don't need transactional detail in two systems.

Table 4.6

COMPARISON OF REVENUE AND COGS SECTION OF CHART OF ACCOUNTS — HORIZONTAL VS VERTICAL METHODOLOGY

Horizontal (use of Classes)	Vertical (use of Divisions)
Sales	Sales
Vodka Sales	Wholesale Sales
Gin Sales	Wholesale Sales: Vodka Sales
Tequila Sales	Wholesale Sales: Gin Sales
Whiskey Sales	Wholesale Sales: Tequila Sales
	Wholesale Sales: Whiskey Sales
	Retail Sales
	Retail Sales: Vodka Sales
	Retail Sales: Gin Sales
	Retail Sales: Tequila Sales
	Retail Sales: Whiskey Sales
COGS	COGS
Gin COGS	Wholesale COGS
Vodka COGS	Wholesale COGS: Gin COGS
Whiskey COGS	Wholesale COGS: Vodka COGS
Mixed Drink COGS	Wholesale COGS: Whiskey COGS
Payroll - Production	Tasting Room COGS
Rent - Production Facility	Tasting Room COGS: Gin COGS
Utilities - Production Facility	Tasting Room COGS: Vodka COGS
Depreciation — Production Equipment	Tasting Room COGS: Whiskey COGS
Excise Tax	Tasting Room COGS: Mixed Drink COGS
	Payroll - Production
	Rent - Production Facility
	Utilities - Production Facility
	Depreciation — Production Equipment
	Excise Tax

As you can see, a fair amount of effort goes into the design of the above-the-line accounts — that is, revenue and COGS accounts. When designing the operating expenses part of the chart of accounts, a manager must keep a similar perspective: how much detail is needed to make informed decisions? What level of resources is available in the accounting department? Will the personnel in the department be able to provide the level of detail sought by management in an accurate and timely fashion?

It's common for companies to overbuild the expense section of the Chart of Accounts. For example, Travel: Meals, Travel: Hotel, Travel: Airfare, and Travel: Cabs may be in the list, when only one Travel account would give sufficient detail. Is the decision maker really going to scrutinize the Cabs expense month-over-month? Or perhaps it's Automobile Expense: Parking, Automobile Expense: Gasoline, Automobile Expense: Maintenance, Automobile Expense: Repairs. Is any of this detailed data practically helpful? I encourage businesses to have one Travel or Automobile Expense account. If the balance in a particular month is large enough to warrant further investigation, the detailed transactions can be extracted by drilling into the account detail. But does management really need that level of detail in the chart of accounts itself? In my experience, this information is not meaningful from the user's perspective.

PULLING REPORTS TO GENERATE THE MOST RELEVANT DATA

There are thousands of ways to present financial information from an accounting database. The information provided on and presentation of reports will differ depending on the audience. Owner/operators may be most concerned with such questions as "Did I make money?", "Am I able to pay upcoming bills?", "How did I do this month vs last month and vs last year?" Employees (if the company is practicing open book management) will have other questions: "Is the company stable?" "Are we doing well?" "What should I expect in the future?" "What is 'normal' for other companies like ours?" Investors will be concerned with return on equity, when they might receive a distribution, and future plans for cash. They will also be concerned with company financial health. Bankers will be concerned with cash flow, ability to pay obligations as they come due, and how leveraged a company is.

Each user may want to see the same information in a different way. Reports should be designed to answer the stakeholders' questions. As a starting point, I recommend that the following reports be reviewed monthly by the senior leadership team:

- Balance Sheet for current period vs last month vs same period last year
- Standard P&L
- Budget vs Actual
- Period-over-Period P&L
- Income Statement by Revenue Center
- Income Statement per Case
- Income Statement with percentage of revenue

Here are a few examples of different ways to present financials in a monthly financial package.

COLLAPSED COMPARATIVE INCOME STATEMENT

This format gives a high-level overview of profitability and displays actual performance versus budget for the month, for the year to date, and for the fiscal year forecast. Note that the rows are different than the presentation of a traditional income statement. For example, operating expenses have been consolidated into two lines: sales/marketing and total overheads and admin cost. There is also a new term on the report: overhead contribution. Overhead contribution measures how much margin is available to cover general and administrative expenses.

The columns in this presentation are a bit different than a traditional income statement. The fiscal year forecast column combines the actual results of the months to date plus the budgeted performance for the following months in the year. The fiscal year budget column is the budgeted performance for all months of the year.

This format is a great lead report for management because it answers the most common questions at a high-level without the burdening the reader with detail. Detailed information should also be provided, but this is a great lead report. *(Table 4.7)*

INCOME PER CE

This version of the collapsed income statement presents figures per case equivalent instead of by total dollar amount. In my experience, one of the best ways to communicate financial data to a non-financial audience is to shift the perspective so that the context is more meaningful to the readers.

This report is presented in case equivalents, but the data can be adapted to proof gallons or any preferred unit of measure. Production staff may resonate with financial data when it references proof gallons, while a salesperson may gravitate toward numbers expressed in case equivalents. *(Table 4.8, see page 40)*

Table 4.7

	Feb Actual	Feb Budget	Variance	YTD Actual	YTD Budget	Variance	FY Forecast	FY Budget	Variance
Revenue	856,344	703,917	152,427	1,604,639	1,390,298	214,241	9.401,513	9.187,272	214,241
Sales Discounts	(104,146)	(42,539)	(61,607)	(168,393)	(90,207)	(78,186)	(734,495)	(656,309)	(78,186)
Net Revenue	752,198	661,378	90,820	1,436,246	1,300,191	136,055	8,667,018	8,530,963	136,055
Total COGS	407,436	479,367	(71,931)	850,281	813,973	36,308	5,404,091	5,367,783	36,308
Gross Margin	344,762	182,011	162,751	585,965	486,218	99,747	3,262,927	3,163,180	99,747
Sales/Marketing	60,656	87,450	(26,794)	117,033	174,900	(57,867)	1,045,533	1,103,400	(57,867)
Overhead Contri-bution	284,106	94,561	189,545	468,932	311,318	157,614	2,217,294	2,059,780	157,614
Total Overheads and Admin Cost	78,562	55,600	22,962	124,863	111,200	13,663	710,863	697,200	13,663
EBITDA	205,544	38,961	166,583	344,069	200,118	143,951	1,506,531	1,362,580	143,951
Interest	856	856	0	1,605	1,605	0	9,402	9,402	0
Taxes	4,282	3,520	762	8,023	6,952	1,071	47,008	45,936	1,071
Depreciation & Amortization	1,713	1,713	0	3,209	3,209	0	18,803	18,803	0
NET INCOME	198,693	32,872	165,872	331,232	188,352	142,880	1,431,319	1,288,439	142,880

Table 4.8

	Feb Actual	Feb Budget	Variance	YTD Actual	YTD Budget	Variance	FY Forecast	FY Budget	Variance
$ / CE									
Revenue	206	197	9	205	211	(6)	212	213	(1)
Sales Discounts	(26)	(6)	(20)	(22)	(43)	21	(15)	(13)	(2)
Net Revenue	180	191	(11)	183	168	15	197	200	(3)
Raw Materials	36	40	(4)	38	39	(1)	40	40	0
Excise Tax	4	4	0	4	4	0	4	4	0
Production Payroll	15	19	(4)	16	17	(1)	17	15	2
Freight	17	25	(8)	19	18	1	20	20	0
Total COGS	72	88	(16)	77	78	(1)	81	79	2
Gross Margin	108	103	5	106	90	16	116	121	(5)
Sales/Marketing	23	31	(8)	23	29	(6)	26	28	(2)
Brand Contribution	85	72	13	83	61	22	90	93	(3)
Total Overheads and Admin Cost	28	26	2	23	11	12	26	21	5
EBITDA	57	46	11	60	50	10	64	72	(8)

Table 4.9

	Feb Actual	Feb Budget	Variance	YTD Actual	YTD Budget	Variance	FY Forecast	FY Budget	Variance
% of Revenue									
Sales Discounts	12%	7%	5%	10%	20%	(10%)	7%	6%	1%
Total COGS	34%	40%	(6%)	36%	37%	(1)	38%	37%	1%
Gross Margin	53%	53%	0%	52%	43%	9%	55%	56%	(1%)
Sales/Marketing	11%	14%	(3%)	11%	12%	(1%)	12%	13%	(1%)
Brand Contribution	42%	39%	3%	41%	31%	10%	43%	43%	0%
Total Overheads and Admin Cost	13%	13%	0%	11%	8%	3%	12%	11%	1%
EBITDA	29%	26%	3%	30%	23%	7%	30%	33%	(3%)

EXPENSE CATEGORIES AS A PERCENTAGE OF REVENUE

Expressing expenses as a percentage of revenue is simple and highly effective for communicating financial information. In this chart, revenue is not stated because it is known to be 100%. Each account line is a percentage of total revenue.

"If you can't measure it, you can't improve it." — Peter Drucker, American management consultant (1909-2005).

Committing to a monthly methodical review of finances is essential. This means doing a line-by-line review of the balance sheet and income statement as well as the abbreviated formats of the income statement shown here, and selected KPIs. The leadership team must be involved so that each department is informed and can make changes within the department to get closer to company goals.

The monthly review is simple and critical. A manager should reserve one hour minimum each month to go line by line and look at the month-over-month change to numbers in each account. What can be learned from the data in each account? Why have increases or decreases occurred? This exercise allows a manager to stay close to the performance of the company. I strongly recommend that time be set aside to review these changes with the leadership team. A well-functioning team has leaders who understand the performance of each division. I recommend that the CFO send reports to all leadership team members at least two days in advance of the team meeting, providing a summary of performance (high level statistics and a few KPIs). In addition to the reports above, monthly review sessions should include liquidity and solvency KPIs, profitability and efficiency KPIs, and review of profitability by SKU.

***AUTHOR'S NOTE** A note to CFOs, accounting managers, or anyone responsible for presenting financial results to the leadership team: each month when you sit around the table and present the prior month's results you are interpreting for the audience the company's financial results. You are painting the picture before the eyes of department heads and managers, and owners. Start by creating an outline (revenue, gross margin, net income/loss, major KPIs), then fill in big blocks of color (product mix, performance by revenue center), finally work on shading and details (highlighting budget overruns, or anomalies in particular accounts). Your summary, high-level reports are the outline, standard reports are the large blocks of color, and detailed reports are the final touches. Focus less on reading the numbers to the audience; instead, point out interesting points in the data and explain what happened. Put yourself in the shoes of the audience and remember that they are not native speakers of the language of finance. Tell a story with the financial information. Draw them into the arc of the story. Finances don't have to be boring, I promise! See yourself as the storyteller and draw in your audience.*

REPORTING RHYTHMS

While the monthly review is the most common cadence for reviewing financials, that does not mean that financial data stays out of sight the other 29 days of the month. A common problem is that business owners or leaders struggle to know which reports they should look at, when and why. Not all financial information needs to be reviewed daily or weekly, but some does. The more frequently data is reviewed, the smaller the amount of data that should be included on the report. It is not the quantity of data, but the right data at the right time that matters.

A manager will determine which data should be reviewed daily, weekly, monthly and boil down reports to be as simple as possible, yet with enough detail to recognize red flags. Here is my suggestion for a reporting rhythm for a small distillery.

Daily report: cash balance. Here are two examples — one with a margin of safety built in, and another without. I recommend keeping at least three months of operating expenses available as margin of safety.

Daily Cash Balance Report March 18, 20XX	
Beginning cash balance	$352,759
Receipts	$43,120
Payments	($73,250)
Ending cash balance	**$322,629**

Daily Cash Balance Report March 18, 20XX	
Beginning cash balance	$352,759
Receipts	$43,120
Payments	($73,250)
Ending cash balance	$322,629
Margin of safety	($300,000)
Available cash balance	**$22,629**

***AUTHOR'S NOTE:** On the daily cash balance report, assume that all outstanding checks have been cashed. Never take your eye off the cash balance.*

Weekly: cash flow forecast, sales and productivity, production *(See Table 4.10)*

***AUTHOR'S NOTE:** Show a two-week projection. There are two categories of inflows: receipt of A/R and credit card deposits. There are 5 categories of outflows: rent, payroll/payroll tax/benefits, general bills, debt service, equipment purchase. Make sure transit time of payments is factored into your assumptions. For example, when do you need to mail a check for it to arrive by the due date?*

Two-Week Cash Flow Snapshot March 18, 20XX		
Week Ending	March 20	March 27
A/R receipts	$43,120	$22,510
Credit card deposits	$38,000	$42,000
Total inflows	**$81,120**	**$64,510**
Rent	$0	$14,000
Payroll, payroll taxes, benefits	$13,300	$0
General expenses	$37,520	$44,100
Debt service	$0	$4,120
Equipment purchases	$12,000	$0
Total outflows	**$62,820**	**$62,220**
Net change in cash	$18,300	$2,290
Beginning cash balance	$302,700	$321,000
Ending cash balance	**$321,000**	**$323,290**

Table 4.10

Sales and Productivity March 18, 20XX					
Period	GM%	Sales	GM$	Cost of Labor	Labor Efficiency Ratio
January	49.5%	$145,000	$71,775	$31,000	$2.32
February	51.2%	$154,000	$78,848	$35,000	$2.25
March					
Week 1	50.0%	$40,000	$20,000	$8,200	$2.44
Week 2	47.6%	$38,000	$18,088	$8,100	$2.23
Week 3					
Week 4					

AUTHOR'S NOTE: Tie in your labor productivity. Labor includes all labor, not just production labor. After identifying what your labor efficiency ratio is, that number won't change much — as long as your business model stays the same.

Production Snapshot March 13, 2021			
Week Ending	3/13/2021	3/15/2020	3/162019
PG produced	500	480	620

Show production in proof gallons for the current week vs same period last year and two years ago.

Monthly: refer to the section on monthly financial review earlier in this chapter. Ideally the books will be closed by the 5th of the month following. This may seem too soon of a turnaround for many businesses, but I have seen it happen successfully in many organizations! The biggest factor leading to a quick close is having a thorough checklist. See the month-end checklist in the Appendix.

USING REPORTS TO ASSESS FINANCIAL HEALTH

Being financially fit means that a company can manage its resources to meet current and long-term needs. Here are keys to financial fitness.

1. Know where you stand. Commit to a monthly methodical review of finances. This process arms company leaders with the information to understand the current situation. Commit to making changes based on the financial review. The biggest value of the review is to help inform changes to be made in operations that move the company closer to where it wants to be.
2. Write a budget. A budget is an incredible management tool that distills values and goals into a practical path forward. It rallies all departments under the same flag and creates buy-in throughout the organization to a singular plan. The budget is a financial expression of the goals and objectives for the coming year. Add the budget to your accounting software. Most software (e.g., Quickbooks, Xero, Orchestrated Spirits) includes a budgeting module and can generate budget vs. actual reports. See chapter seven for an in-depth discussion of budgets.
3. Keep positive cash flow. The spirits industry is seasonal, and some slow months may have negative cash flow, but overall cash flow should be positive for the year. With liquid assets increasing, debt can be repaid, cash can be reinvested into the business, profits can be returned to shareholders, and there is a cash safety net. Understand the difference between cash flow and profitability and always protect cash.
4. Keep debt in check. There is good debt and there is bad debt. Good debt has the potential to increase net worth; for example, a mortgage or an SBA loan at favorable terms. Bad debt is borrowed money used to fuel working capital; for example, credit card debt. Bad debt suggests that the business model is not sustainable.
5. Evaluate each business center on its own merits. For example, if your operation has wholesale sales, retail sales, and a restaurant, then it will be most helpful to see the performance of each center. A restaurant is a completely different business model than wholesale sales, and performance should be judged accordingly.

Real-Life Application

WHALEN INSURANCE

Insurance is a cornerstone for any business, but it is of critical importance for distilleries. Peter Whalen is an insurance professional who has specialized in beverage alcohol for decades. His agency, Whalen Insurance is located in Massachusetts. We sat down to discuss the fundamentals of insurance for distillers.

Insurance is what keeps people from bankruptcy after they have a loss. A distillery can create the safest workplace possible but despite that, things can happen. Some of my biggest claims have been in businesses where I thought this couldn't happen, but then there was an accident. Very few businesses can handle a fire claim, for example.

One thing that I think people don't appreciate is business interruption insurance. Sometimes they have enough insurance on other fronts, but not enough business interruption coverage. Business interruption insurance is critical because it takes care of any ongoing expenses such as debt service, utilities, and key personnel salaries. It even covers profits that would have been earned in the covered period. The amount of recommended coverage for business interruption depends on the total disaster's claim and how long would it take you to rebuild after a significant event. For example, let's assume a distillery has $100,000 in expenses per month. If there were a fire or other event, there will be some expenses that don't recur while the supplier is not operational. For illustration purposes we'll assume that the recurring expenses lowers to $50,000 per month. If it takes the business a year to recover, that would be a $600,000 annual policy. [$50,000 per month times 12 months]

A distillery can be an expensive endeavor! Very few people can afford to have a large investment at risk. When you consider the cost to build a facility – let's say $1 million – plus the years of financial contribution as you distill, barrel, and age your product. Over a five year period needed to age whiskey, a company may have invested $5 million. You can see why it's critical to have that asset properly insured.

For distillers, fire is the biggest risk. You can put a fire out with beer, you can't with whiskey. There are some basic precautions: you must have the proper ventilation system and sprinkler system. This is unique to distillers; a restaurant or a retail store doesn't encounter the same exposure. A good portion of a distiller's operation is creating a fire hazard. It's the explosiveness and the flammability of liquor that sets the industry apart. It's a unique industry to service and not every insurance agent will be able to meet those unique needs.

I'm often asked what adequate coverage is for a supplier. In my opinion, it's full replacement value of the operation. If a manufacturer has a major claim, they will not have the luxury of time to find the best deal on equipment; they need to buy equipment as quickly as possible. Assume you will need to replace equipment at today's value, not the historical cost. It's important to get operations up and running as quickly as possible.

There is no rule of thumb of how much coverage a distiller should have for business interruption coverage. The standard for liability coverage is $1 million per occurrence, $2 million aggregate, per year.

After purchasing basic coverage, umbrella policies are available, which can provide additional layers of protection. I have a lot of clients who have up to $10 million umbrella coverage, but they usually generate $30 million in annual revenues.

Another aspect that makes distilleries unique is the aging process. This can be a huge exposure. Let's say someone is making a high end whiskey they are going to age for 4 years. They barrel it and put it in a rickhouse. At that moment it's worth $700; upon aging it's worth $5,000. What happens if a fire hits at three years and eleven months? Distillers need to make sure that coverage goes up as time goes on. Coverage cost (premium) will be set at a value that's in the middle (beginning value vs end value), or you can expect it to increase in cost as time passes.

One word of wisdom it to separate inventory into tranches so that if a fire breaks out, it's not going to destroy the entire inventory. The reason why insurance companies have run away from the distilling industry is because these businesses have more exposure in terms of fire, explosions, and death, than many companies are willing to insure. Industry-wide there have been many disasters.

When interviewing insurance agents, distillers should deal with someone who knows what they are doing. People say, "I have this local insurance agent that I love, but when I mention I'm opening a distillery you could tell that the person is clueless. I have no confidence who knows what he's doing." When it comes to insuring your business – and possibly your life's savings - it's important to get it right. People don't like insurance. It's expensive, it's incomprehensible. So, they deal with it as little as possible. But it's so important for a business owner to deal with it initially and put together an adequate policy. And working with someone who knows what they are talking about makes the process infinitely easier. Spend the time up front to make sure that your insurance program will cover you adequately so that you are going to be okay when the disaster hits.

CHAPTER **FIVE**

Understanding Cost Concepts and Breakeven

FINANCIAL ACCOUNTING VS COST ACCOUNTING

When most people think of accounting it is seen as black-and-white with very little room for different points of view or approaches. In reality, there are many approaches to accounting. It is true, in the United States there is a standard set of rules: GAAP, or generally accepted accounting principles. GAAP is quite useful because it provides a common framework that different companies can adopt, and from which judgments can be made about the performance of one company versus another.

But accounting has a much broader palate than that one set of rules. The principles of accounting can be applied to serve different applications. Two common types of accounting are financial accounting and cost accounting. Financial accounting involves preparing financial reports according to a framework (usually GAAP) for the benefit of outside stakeholders such as investors, the public, or lenders. Cost accounting involves applying accounting principles to produce reports that are useful from a managerial perspective.

Cost accounting focuses on accurately capturing the cost of a good manufactured so that accurate sales price can be determined. This is vitally important because without accurately tracking *all* costs of an item, management will not know the profitability of what has been sold. Without this information, management cannot determine if a specific item is profitable or if the current product mix is sustainable.

Cost accounting and managerial accounting are very similar and the terms are often used interchangeably. In this text we will use the term cost accounting. It is used internally by management to make fully informed business decisions. Cost accounting captures a company's total cost of production by assessing the variable costs of each step of production as well as fixed costs, such as a lease expense. A variable cost stays the same per unit produced, but increases in aggregate. A fixed cost does not change regardless of the number of units produced, but on a per-unit basis the cost decreases with each additional unit produced. Cost accounting doesn't have to follow the same rules as GAAP, unlike financial accounting which does follow a standardized set of rules. Financial accounting is used to present the performance of a company to outside parties. GAAP excludes selling and administrative costs for inventory valuation. Cost accounting is not required to adhere to set standards and can be flexible to meet the needs of management. One example of how the two differ is in the classification of expenses. Cost accounting includes all input costs associated with production, and can be classified as variable, fixed, direct or indirect costs.

A fully costed product includes labor and overhead. These items - payroll, rent, etc — normally show up on the income statement. When these costs are included in inventory, they move *off* the income statement and *onto* the balance sheet. Consider the effects of this shift on barrel-aged product. If a whiskey ages for several years, then a large amount of indirect costs can end up in the inventory. The company does not, then, get the tax benefit of the expense until that barrel-aged product is sold well into the future. This is one example of a distillery as a capital-intensive business. The producer does not receive revenue of barrel-aged goods until several years after the cash expenditures for the goods are made. The distillery must rely on capital contributions (or debt) to fund the operation until the aged spirit is ready for sale.

***AUTHOR'S NOTE** Cost accounting is also helpful in obtaining accurate insurance coverage. If you have coverage for lost product or business interruption, and if your inventory is undervalued when applying for your insurance policy, then your coverage will likely be insufficient to cover the entire cost if you need to make a claim.*

COST ACCOUNTING KEY CONCEPTS

Cost accounting captures a company's total cost of production by assessing the variable costs of each step of production as well as fixed costs, such as lease expense.

- Cost accounting, management accounting
  These terms are very similar and often used interchangeably. In this text we use "cost accounting."
- Financial accounting vs cost accounting
  Financial accounting provides financial information in a standardized and regimented format (most commonly GAAP). Financial accounting is used to present the performance of a company to outside parties. Cost accounting is not required to adhere to set standards and can be flexible to meet the needs of management.
- Different classification of expenses
  Cost accounting includes all input costs associated with production, and can be classified as variable, fixed, direct or indirect costs.

COSTING METHODS

Businesses use costing methods to determine the price of a product and to analyze the efficiency of resource consumption. These methods often comply with the external financial reporting rules set forth by GAAP, which require all manufacturing costs, including overhead, to be assigned to goods in inventory for costing purposes. However, companies can internally use alternative costing methods that do not comply with GAAP. To identify the most beneficial costing method for a company's circumstances, it's important to understand how each method calculates cost of product. Then management can weigh each costing method's advantages and disadvantages along with circumstances that help dictate the use of each method to find the most appropriate method for the company.

There are several costing methods, including standard costing, activity-based costing, lean accounting, and marginal costing. Ultimately, the method chosen should be appropriate for the size and scope of the operation and a reasonable balance of cost-benefit. That is, it should not be a calculation so complicated that all benefit of the detail is outweighed by the cost of actually making the calculation.

STANDARD COSTING

A budgeted amount is assigned to each element of an item's production process, resulting in a budgeted, or standard, total cost per unit. Each component of an item's recipe, or bill of materials, is assigned an expected, standard, cost. Expected costs are also assigned for direct labor, overhead, and other direct expenses (e.g., excise taxes). At period-end, the actual cost of an item (actual costs paid by the company for production) is compared to the standard cost that was expected. Variances are related to the difference of either (a) quantity of input used or (b) unit cost of input.

A standard cost system provides easier inventory valuation than an actual cost system. Under an actual cost system, unit costs for batches of identical products may differ widely. *(Table 5.1)*

ACTIVITY BASED COSTING

Activity based costing assigns costs differently than the standard cost method. Direct and indirect costs are assigned to each unit sold in a period based on the total production for the period. Each activity of the production cycle is defined (distilling, cellaring, bottling, canning, kegging). Then the cost of those activities is allocated to the relevant products. For example, bottling labor costs would only be allocated to the bottled finished goods items produced in a period. *(Table 5.2)*

Assume the following: a distillery produces 1,000 PG in a month. 750 PG is clear vodka; 250 PG is flavored vodka. Labor expense categories include hourly and salaried labor for distilling, flavoring, bottling, packaging, and warehouse.

To allocate costs, clear vodka gets 75% of all costs except flavoring labor. It gets none of those items. Clear vodka therefore gets $14,625 of labor allocated to it.

$22,000 - $2,500 flavoring labor = $19,500 X 75% = $14,625.

Flavored vodka gets 25% of all costs except flavoring labor. Flavoring labor is 100% attributed to the flavored vodka.

Table 5.1

Costs	Standard Cost per CE	Planned Cost per Year	Actual Cost per Year	Variance ($)
Planned production		***2,000 CE***	***1,800 CE***	***(200 CE)***
Raw Materials	$7.92	$15,840	$13,780	($2,060)
Packaging	$37.32	$74,640	$68,669	($5,971)
Distilling Labor	$2.00	$4,000	$4,400	$400
Packaging Labor	$1.05	$2,010	$2,200	$190
Utilities and Supplies per Hour of Labor	$4.15	$8,300	$8,200	($100)
Rent		$12,000	$12,000	$0
Total		$116,790	$109,249	($7,541)

Table 5.2

Labor Expenses	Total	Classic Vodka	Flavored Vodka
PG produced	***1,000***	***750***	***250***
Distilling - Hourly	$3,000	$2,250	$750
Distilling - Salaried	$4,000	$3,000	$1,000
Flavoring - Hourly	$500		$500
Flavoring - Salaried	$2,000		$2,000
Bottling - Hourly	$2,500	$1,875	$625
Packaging - Salaried	$5,000	$3,750	$1,250
Warehouse -Salaried	$5,000	$3,750	$1,250
Total Labor Expense	$22,000	$14,625	$7,375
Total Labor / PG		$19.50	$29.50

Table 5.3

Lean Costing Income Statement	
Revenue	$100,000
Cost of Sales	
Purchases	$9,250
(Increase)/decrease in direct material inventory	($1,000)
Total Material Costs	$8,250
Processing Costs	
Distilling Labor	$22,000
Distilling Employee Benefits	$1,800
Distilling Supplies	$9,000
Distilling equipment depreciation	$25,000
Total Processing Costs	$57,800
Occupancy Costs	
Rent	$12,000
Total Occupancy Costs	$12,000
Total Manufacturing Costs	$78,050
(Increase)/decrease in overhead	$10,000
Total Cost of Sales	$88,050
Gross Margin	$11,950

$19,500 - $14,625 = $4,875 + $2,500 = $7,375.

Activity based costing provides a more accurate method of product costing, leading to more accurate pricing decisions. It increases understanding of overheads and cost drivers; and makes costly and non-value adding activities more visible, allowing managers to reduce or eliminate them.[1]

LEAN ACCOUNTING

The primary goal of lean accounting is to eliminate waste and produce just enough to meet customer demand. Costs are organized by value stream. Value stream is the chain of events that create value for a customer while producing a product. Costs are organized by value stream and no distinction is made between direct or indirect costs — all costs of the value stream are considered direct costs. Value stream costs include labor, materials, production support, machines and equipment, operation support, facilities and maintenance. Value stream costing is beneficial because it highlights unnecessary costs outside the control of value stream managers. *(Table 5.3)*

MARGINAL COSTING

In marginal costing only the variable costs associated with a product are included in the calculation of a product's contribution margin. This method ignores fixed costs over a relevant range. Only variable costs are considered. Examples of variable costs include the raw materials, packaging items, hourly labor, and excise tax. *(Table 5.4)*

The advantages of marginal costing are that it is easy to operate and simple to understand. Marginal costing is useful in profit planning because it clearly shows profitability at different levels of production and sales. It is useful in decision making about fixation of selling price and make-or-buy decisions.

Break-even analysis and price/volume ratio are useful techniques of marginal costing. Evaluation of different departments is possible through marginal costing. Under marginal costing, valuation of inventory is done at marginal cost; therefore, it is not possible to carry forward illogical fixed overheads from one accounting period to the next period.

Table 5.4

Income Statement (marginal costing method)	
Sales	$100,000
Variable Costs	
Cost of Goods Sold	($35,000)
Variable Selling Expenses	($12,000)
Variable Admin Expenses	($13,000)
Contribution Margin	**$40,000**
Fixed Costs	
Fixed Selling Expenses	($15,000)
Fixed Admin Expenses	($15,000)
Net Income	**$10,000**

When choosing a costing method there are a few considerations:

1. Does the costing method comply with the type of product the firm generates? For example, many homogenous products (such as one brand of vodka – high volume, low specialization), or few products that are different (such as unique aged spirits - low volume, high specialization).
2. Does it provide the desired degree of accuracy?
3. Can it be implemented with the resources available to the company?
4. Other considerations: Does the costing method provide enough information to allow management to make an informed decision about the true cost of a product, and therefore the appropriate sales price for that product?

THE IMPORTANCE OF COSTING

The sales price of an item is usually set with consideration of the cost to produce that item. A sales price has a ceiling, which is set by the market. There

1 1CGMA - www.cgma.org/resources/tools/essential-tools/activity-based-costing

is a certain value as perceived by the customer above which the customer will not purchase the good. The sales price floor should be the cost to produce an item.* A business can either overcharge or under-charge for an item, and under-charging is much more economically damaging than overcharging. If a customer purchases an underpriced item, real dollars are lost on the amount of COGS that exceed the revenue.

***AUTHOR'S NOTE:* *I emphasize *should* in this sentence because I see loss leaders hit the market quite often. A loss leader is a product sold at a loss to attract customers. The theory is that when a customer buys a loss leader, he or she will buy another product with a healthy margin. In my experience, when a company sells a SKU at a loss it is not because they intend to do so. They do it because their costing data is not detailed enough to see clearly to cost of each product!**

Because sales price is often based on cost, it is critical to have a solid costing method in place for all goods. Only when the sales price is set appropriate to the item's cost will a business have profit. Once costs are known, the distillery sets the sales price.

MARK-UP VS MARGIN

Mark-up and margin are two terms used when discussing how to price goods. They are similar but different concepts.

Mark-up is the percentage increase added to the cost of a good.

Margin is the sales price minus COGS.

If shelf price is $30 after a 50% markup, the price to retailer is $20.

1.5X = $30

X = $30/1.5

X = $20

If shelf price is $30 and the price to retailer is $20, then the margin is 33%.

$30 - $20 = $10

$10/$30 = 33%

To calculate mark-up or margin, start with the shelf price and work backwards from there. Shelf price is usually the same, regardless of whether the product is sold to a consumer from the manufacturer or from a retailer. Consider the desired profit margin of the retailer. Shelf price less the desired retailer profit margin equals PTR (price to retailer). If a producer is not selling through a wholesaler, price to retailer is the distiller's sales price. In that scenario PTR - COGS = margin.

For example, assume a $30 shelf price with 50% markup. The producer's revenue is $20. If the producer requires 40% margin, then costs are $12/unit. ($20 - (60%*$20) = $20 - $12 = $8 margin

If a producer is selling through a wholesaler, PTR is the wholesaler's sales price. To calculate a supplier's margin in this scenario you have to account for that third tier properly. Follow this formula:

Shelf price - PTR - wholesaler's margin (generally 30%) = FOB pricing. FOB - COGS = distiller's margin.

FOB stands for freight on board. The term indicates when liability of a product shifts from one party to another. In the context of beverage alcohol sales, FOB refers to the sales price of a good from a supplier to a wholesaler.

The section above describes the quantitative analysis including in setting a price, but there is much more qualitative analysis involved. In reality, establishing a price point for goods is equal parts art and science. Look at the competitive landscape and determine the sales price of other similar goods in your sales markets. Consider the brand and its position in your portfolio (well, premium, super-premium). For more insight on price setting strategies, see the commentary from Chris Joseph, CEO of Cascade Spirits, in chapter eight.

CHAPTER **SIX**

Different Business Models

A business model is a structure for business operations. It involves identifying revenue streams, setting a plan for buying or creating the good or service that is sold, and management of the operation. To manage the operation, leaders rely on industry financial benchmarks. For example, grocery stores sell tangible goods and have very low margins. On the other hand, law firms sell services and have very high margins. These businesses represent two very different models.

Within the distilled spirits industry, there are various business models. Perhaps the most traditional is the wholesale model. In this model, a producer sells product to a distributor (wholesaler). The wholesaler sells it to a retailer, and the retailer sells it to the end user. This model alleviates the need for the producer to transport its product to multiple different retailers (liquor stores, grocery stores, bars, restaurants), so it simplifies the producer's operations. However, this convenience comes at a price: generally a distributor takes 30% of the price to retailer, so the producer makes less revenue on wholesale sales than they would if they sold directly to the retailer.

Another business model is self-distribution. Self-distribution is governed by state laws; in some states a distillery can sell directly to a retailer; in other states they cannot.

Let's compare the economics of both models, assuming a case sells for $320 to a retailer.

If using a third-party distributor:

$320 price to retail — 30% to distributor = $X revenue to producer

$320 = 1.3X

$246 = X. $246 is the revenue per case to the producer.

If selling directly to retailer, the producer would make $320 per case. Therefore, self-distribution yields $74 more revenue per case than a third-party distributor.

Seems like a no-brainer. Why would any company

use a distributor if the option to self-distribute was available? Well, fulfilling distribution is a complex and costly endeavor, and it becomes more complex the larger a producer becomes.

In fact, managing a distribution operation requires a different skillset than managing distillery operations. When a company adds distribution to their model, it will be an investment. Distributing product requires vehicles, distribution labor, vehicle maintenance and fuel costs. These all quickly add up. Additionally, the logistics are quite cumbersome if covering several points of distribution and/or a large geographic area. To think that managing one's own distribution will add 30% to the bottom line is incorrect — there are significant additional costs to bear. True, a supplier may come out ahead, financially, with self-distribution, but as with many other business decisions I caution owners to do a cost-benefit analysis before launching into it.

Another common business model is the tasting room. In this model the producer sells his own goods onsite in a bar environment. He may also sell bottles to go. The drawback to this model is that the revenue is limited by the physical location. A tasting room will be open no more than 7 days a week for a certain number of hours per day and with a certain number of seats. Even if a tasting room were open 24/7/365, there would still be a revenue cap due to the limitations of the physical space. Tasting rooms are more labor intensive than a wholesale operation, and if a supplier is operating a full service restaurant, the labor expense can be three to four times the amount that it would be to support the simplified operations of a tasting room. Sales through a tasting room are the most lucrative of all sales channels. There is no middleman between producer and end user. The patron pays full price for goods, and no margin is taken out along the way from production to end consumer. Tasting room operations are not allowed in all states, so this may not be an option for all readers.

Another retail sales channel is direct-to-consumer sales (DTC). Technically, tasting room sales are direct to consumer, but the term DTC has been used in the beverage alcohol business to denote online sales. The laws for selling alcoholic beverages online depend on the laws of the state of the producer (and of the purchaser). DTC sales can be lucrative and can broaden the customer base, but this sales channel is also legally complicated and logistically challenging. (See the commentary from Ryan Thompson of 10th Mountain Distillery for more insights on the DTC landscape.)

***AUTHOR'S NOTE:** Since the COVID-19 pandemic hit in early 2020, creative solutions for getting products into the hands of consumers have blossomed. As the saying goes, necessity is the mother of invention. During the pandemic many third-party fulfillment companies improved logistics, and many states have relaxed rules (many of them permanent changes) related to sales of alcohol direct to consumers. It is interesting to watch how changes to the regulatory environment will play out as we country moves forward. I, for one, believe these small changes to regulation are kicking the door open to vastly change how business is done in the world of distilled spirits.*

But every debate has more than one perspective. Changes to the regulatory landscape may not all be in the best interest of suppliers. The regulated environment theoretically levels the playing field for producers of all sizes. How might business change if, for example, slotting fees became the normal course of business. The world of beverage alcohol would start to resemble the world of non-alcoholic beverage, which has much slimmer margins. There is a limit to the additional expenses that a producer can absorb. The future of beverage alcohol regulation is currently shifting and there are many uncertainties, but most producers agree that the momentum of the DTC movement is far from over.

A popular option for start-up distilleries is to use contract distillers. This is yet another business model option. A spirits company can be structured as, essentially, a marketing company. The company creates the idea, brands the product, finds the market, sells the product — assume all business functions except for production. A separate — usually, larger — producer manufactures and packages the liquor. This business model allows a company to get started without the significant capital investments required for full operations. It lessens the amount of cash required for start-up, allowing time to prove a concept while minimizing financial risk.

Perhaps the most attractive aspect of this business model is that a company can demand a higher value if equity is raised at a future date. The enterprise value — the value that is used when raising money — of an investment in a nascent company will be much less than the enterprise value of a proven, operational company. When investing in a start-up, a buyer receives a substantial discount for the risk involved, and as the company matures, that risk declines and the investment becomes more valuable.

As you probably know, aged spirits generally take a minimum of four years to mature. Many distilleries will want to sell aged spirits as soon as the company is operational. In other words, they don't want to wait four years to generate revenue. In these situations the distiller may choose to purchase two or more aged spirits produced by a different company, create their own proprietary blend, and sell the blended aged product. Of course this business model is more costly than a traditional model in which the company waits for wash to age, but it allows a pathway for immediate revenue.

***AUTHOR'S NOTE:** Over the years I have seen the contract distilling model grow in popularity for start-ups. In most cases a company will turn a corner and sales will reach a point where it makes sense economically to switch from a contract manufacturing model to a traditional model in which the company makes their own spirits. However, I have seen plenty of distilleries continue with a contract manufacturing model well into the maturity of the company.*

Hone in on the core competencies of your organization. If your company has fantastic branding and marketing skills, but little experience in actually crafting a spirit, then the contract manufacturing arrangement is perfect! The key to successful business is to refine your greatest strength and outsource the rest.

I've encountered many purists in the alcohol beverage industry who believe a 'real' company makes their own product. I understand that point of view, but it's a little short-sighted. A company can still be wildly successful even if some components of the process are outsourced. Consider the opposite: if a distillery has great production skills but mediocre branding skills, then it will hire an outside marketing firm. This is a common business practice, and the result is that the outside firm backfills some competencies needed for a successful business. Don't limit your options by buying into perceived barriers.

Generally, a spirits company will use a combination of more than one business model. Because each business model has different benchmarks, it becomes important to separate these lines through the use of classes or divisions in the accounting system.

Inevitably, the economic situation of a company and an industry will change. Businesses need to understand the structure of various business models so that they can pivot accordingly. Some market forces change slowly and steadily, like the public's preference for spirits over beer, for example. Other market forces change quickly and without warning, like the COVID-19 pandemic's effect on the regulatory environment.

PIVOTING

A business owner must be ready to change direction on short notice. As our industry is changing rapidly, managing through this environment requires a unique combination of short-term planning and long-range sensibilities.

When a business owner senses that the environment is shifting, he must take precautions and be prepared. First, the owner must establish the habit of reviewing the financial position and financial forecast on a regular basis. The more volatile the environment, the more frequently oversight is needed.

He must be aware of opportunities and threats, and consider how to manage them. For example, if tasting room sales cease, as was the case for most of proprietors during COVID-19, how will that lost revenue be backfilled? Perhaps the instinct is to cut expenses so that there is minimal impact to net income. Another option might be to permanently close the tasting room and focus every effort on wholesale. I encourage every business to have at the ready two or three alternative scenarios to act upon on short notice.

Many business owners can feel paralyzed when trying to forecast for the future, but I truly believe with a cash flow forecast tool in hand, there are few unknowns that can't be uncovered. Keep asking questions to understand why a cost behaves the way it does. Continuing that process long enough can usually create a reasonable estimation of future financial performance.

The idea of creating a financial model may sound daunting and complex, but it doesn't have to be. Modeling simply means that a new set of assumptions is cost over an existing forecast. For example, a company has an annual budget by month. It may decide mid-year to model the impact of bringing and ready-to-drink cocktail to market. The finance team does not need to start from scratch; they will simply take the existing budget and update the affected accounts in the affected months.

Finally, being proactive in making hard choices is important. Many business owners prolong difficult conversations or choices, but once the necessary action is clear, they should move forward swiftly with those changes. A lot of time and money can be wasted in procrastination.

Having a well-considered plan will allow an owner to move quickly and effectively, keeping business nimble in this erratic environment.

Tenets to being nimble:

- Be ready to change direction on short notice.
- Review your financial position and financial forecast on a weekly basis. The more volatile the environment, the more frequently oversight is needed.
- Model different scenarios. Consider two or three alternative scenarios. Create a financial model for each and update each at least monthly.
- Be proactive in making hard choices.

In addition to having a couple of alternative plans at your disposal at any time, companies should periodically take stock of their business terms. Here are some suggestions for improving the terms, and thus, financial results of your business. Some of the suggestions are easy changes that can make a big difference. Try updating these items first before changing your entire operations.

1. Consider updating your credit terms. If you have accounts receivable, do you have room to shorten the payment period? If payment is due 30 days after invoice date, can you change that to Net 15 terms — meaning that payment is due 15 days after invoice date? Remember, there is no reason why you cannot change your credit policies. Accounting policies should not be changed sporadically and without good reason, but accounting policies should be reviewed periodically to ensure that they still serve the organization's needs.
2. Draw down your inventory. Create a target level of inventory based on sales in a future period. For example, if you have an average production cycle of two weeks, your inventory on hand should map to the sales two weeks into the future plus a small amount extra as a safety net. A challenge for distillers, particularly those making brown spirits, is the long production cycle. This can make planning very tricky, and target levels of inventory on hand are difficult to define. As a barrel is harvested, finished goods on hand will increase and will deplete with sales. Producers of brown spirits will need either to create separate target levels of inventory for aged vs non-aged products, or to define an acceptable range of inventory on hand that takes into account the high inventory when a barrel is initially bottled.
3. Consider lowering the order quantity of direct materials to support a healthier cash flow. Many small businesses become concerned with maximizing net income, when they would be better served maximizing cash flow. I often see brewery owners enter a contract for packaging materials that requires a large order quantity because the per-unit price is favorable, but they forget that it requires a substantial outlay of cash. Sometimes it is better to pay a little more per unit and preserve your cash balance.

Real-Life Application

RYAN THOMPSON, TENTH MOUNTAIN DISTILLERY

My experience in the world of distilling was an organic progression. I first moved to Vail in 1998 and bartended for four years. From there I started a restaurant and ran it for 15 years. I saw what the craft distillery movement was doing. It seemed to follow the craft beer movement by about ten years or so. I thought that someone in this town was going to make whiskey soon enough and I thought, "it might as well be me." At the same time, I'd been homebrewing as a hobby, and decided to learn how to distill. I took some courses on distilling in Kentucky, then wrote a business plan, found some investors, and here we are today! It's been eight years that Tenth Mountain has been in business. We incorporated in 2013, and became operational in 2014. We built the distillery first, then opened a tasting room in Vail Village, and then about a year later opened the second tasting room at our production facility.

We signed on with a distributor about six months after opening the first tasting room. We were aware of the economics of working with a distributor — the fact that they take 30% of the margin to retailer. (We had been self-distributing in our immediate vicinity — and we still do — so we had an idea of what the numbers were like when distributing on our own. Self-distribution works well for us in this area because our sales team pretty much knows everyone in town, certainly in the bar and restaurant industry.) The numbers weren't a shock. What was a shock is how little the distributors care about you. You think once they get you in their book, they will actually sell your product, but they don't. A distributor's job is to take you from Point A to Point B and they don't necessarily sell unless you are keeping their lights on, like a Jack Daniel's or a Jim Beam. Now we've been with our Colorado distributor for seven years. During that time we have developed a relationship and have started to do programming with them, so there's more of a partnership now when it comes to sales. We're starting to get some decent traction in Colorado, but it's taken a while.

We brought on a National Sales Director about two years ago and it has been a game-changer to have him on the streets and work side-by-side with distributors. Looking back on it, we might have brought on a sales manager at the same time as signing with a distributor. I don't think there's a reason to bring on a distributor unless you can support that distributor in that market with a sales person. One thing I'd like to reinforce about working with distributors in far locations is that you really have to be prepared for the financial investment. The ability to fly there, rent a car, stay in hotel rooms for multiple weeks, and work with your distributor is essential. As long as you can support those sales with your own sales personnel, go for it.

We also do direct-to-consumer sales with a third party. We started DTC sales about five years ago, and in that time we've worked with three fulfillment partners. There are a lot of lessons learned for Tenth Mountain about how to select the right partner. My short list of considerations includes:

(1) confirm whether you own the buyer's contact information;

(2) know the number of states that the fulfillment company can sell to;

(3) understand the third party's fee structure;

(4) be prepared to factor in the shipping fees. Margin is good with DTC sales, but you do need to remember that shipping is an extra cost and logistical consideration. Digital marketing is also an important part of selling online. We have a full-time person who focuses solely on digital marketing. I advise other distilleries not to go into online sales without a budget for social media campaigns.

I think it's smart to operate in multiple business models. The tasting rooms offer the face-to-face contact and the opportunity to convert patrons to lifelong fans and ambassadors. The online model allows you to connect with buyers around the country who otherwise would not be aware of your brand. And, finally, you can't ignore the traditional three-tier market. That's the way things always have been and it's not going away. If I had to choose only one, right now it would be the tasting-room model. But in a few years, it would be the DTC model. That's because I believe that in a few years all the state laws will change to allow uninhibited interstate commerce for spirits. Once we turn that corner, I think the direct-to-consumer sales channel will outpace any other spoke on the wheel.

Other recommendations for financial health are to have a really good CPA and to watch the numbers! I watch my Profit and Loss really closely. I look at it year-to-date and the trailing twelve months, paying close attention to expense percentages relative to revenue. And I watch cash like a hawk! Keeping close to your finances will keep you out of trouble.

Ryan Thompson, Founder and CEO
Tenth Mountain Distillery

4. Look at secondary markets as a source of inventory purchases. When on-premise sales dried up during the COVID-19 pandemic, many businesses offloaded excess raw materials on secondary exchanges. These secondary market outlets can be a great way to pick up inventory at a lower cost and lower quantity than you might get from traditional outlets.
5. Attach margin to everything you sell. This is no time for loss leaders. Do you have a clear idea of how much each brand of spirit contributes in gross margin? It's worthwhile to do the exercise and understand just how much you are making on your core styles, and also the difference in margin by pack type.
6. Consider innovation. How can you use innovation in order to thrive through a changing environment? Are there emerging techniques or practices thatyou can implement. For example, are you making your own whiskey wash? Could you buy it from a neighboring brewery for less than what it would cost to make it yourself?
7. Analyze your value chain and identify opportunities to automate and create efficiency. The value chain is the production, marketing, and service of making and selling your spirits. It starts with the suppliers from whom you purchase raw materials, through to your distributors and salespeople. Are there any points that can be refined to give you more profit?
8. Finally, perhaps our greatest opportunity for innovation relates to the regulatory environment, as noted above. The world's response to COVID-19 resulted in shutting down on-premise sales channels for an undetermined timeline. Additionally, the economic repercussions of the pandemic have resulted in consumers having less disposable income, but we do have the chance to make changes in our regulatory environment and the three-tier system. Many states have relaxed rules and made permanent changes to sell direct to consumer. We have before us the best chance in history to make changes to the restrictive three-tier system.

MAP OUT YOUR STRATEGY

In today's environment you can't assume that your current business model is infallible. The pace of change in the industry is unprecedented. Those with the best access to business data - and the ability to analyze it - will win. Creative problem solving will win.

Always think a few chess moves ahead and have multiple options for the next course of action. For example, if you foresee capacity restraints, you might have the following options:

a. Buy more equipment or build a new facility
b. Find a contract brewer who can make more of your product
c. Keep supply unchanged but increase the sales price
d. Cut production of less profitable brands and sell more of more profitable brands

Create a financial model for each scenario in order to see the financial effects of each option and make an informed decision on how to proceed.

SOLVING PROBLEMS THROUGH FINANCIAL MODELING

Financial modeling can be extremely helpful when problem solving in business. To solve a problem, follow these steps:

1. Define the problem
2. Do a SWOT analysis. (SWOT is short for strengths, weaknesses, opportunities, threats)
3. Identify multiple solutions
4. Create a financial model for each possible solution

Framing a course of action in financial terms is helpful because the model will expose in quantitative terms whether the plan is viable. The process of financial modeling expresses a plan in financial terms. There are three basic steps to the process: gather historical data, define assumptions, and create forecasted financial results.

The greater period of historical data available for

the model, the better, but generally the trailing twelve months' data is the minimum required. Twenty-four months is preferable. To begin, start with the historical balance sheet, historical income statement and historical statement of cash flows — all by month. Build a workbook in Excel in which each financial statement should have its own tab.

***AUTHOR'S NOTE:** One caveat — if historical period data is questionable in its accuracy, it will not be helpful in your forecasting. Also, if there were structural changes to the organization that make the historical data obsolete, then either omit it or be sure to account for that structural change in your calculation of future periods. An example is historical sales data. If you sold only vodka and gin in prior periods, but you now will be selling whiskey, then you should accommodate for that difference in future periods. It will not suffice to simply multiply prior period sales by the assumed growth rate. Instead, you will multiply prior periods by assumed growth rate (for vodka and gin) and add an additional amount for sales of whiskey.*

Second, define assumptions for future periods. How will each line item of the balance sheet, income statement, and statement of cash flows behave under the scenario you are modeling? Create a separate tab for your assumptions. The assumptions tab will include input cells that will link to formulas on the forecast tabs. Design the forecast workbook so that the number of manual input cells is minimized. This will reduce the opportunity for human error. On the forecasted tabs, formulas will dictate the results in the cells, and the formulas will be driven by the assumptions. For example, if projected sales growth is hard keyed in the assumptions tab at 5%, then the forecasted sales cells will reference back to that cell in the assumptions tab that shows 5% growth rate.

***AUTHOR'S NOTE:** There are plenty of software programs that will create future models based on historical data. It doesn't have to all be done manually.*

Consider the ratios in historical information as well as expected behavior in future periods. Create assumptions for — at minimum, product margins, growth rates, and asset turnover.

Third, create forecasted financial results. This is where assumptions about future performance are compiled. The result is a set of pro forma financials - forecasted financial statements that show the outcome of a particular set of assumptions. Forecasting monthly for one year into the future is a good rule of thumb. The further into the future forecasts are projected, the less reliable they become. If forecasting beyond one year, consider forecasting by quarter instead of by month.

While forecasts are extremely helpful to narrow down which future course of action is best, financial metrics alone fall short of capturing a company's total value. Indeed, non-financial measures of performance should also be considered before proceeding with a course of action. Whereas financial goals are focused on short-term periods, non-financial measures reflect how a potential project will align with a company's values or long term goals. Common non-financial metrics include quality, customer and employee satisfaction, and innovation. Examples of questions that non-financial metrics can help answer include:

Quality

- If a project is pursued, how much money is expected to be spent on warranties?
- What is the total expense of the customer service department?
- What is the product defect percentage?
- What is the on-time rate? That is, the percentage of time products are completed on schedule.

Customer and employee satisfaction

- What is the customer or employee retention rate?
- How satisfied are your customers? We strongly recommend measuring customer satisfaction in some way so that you have a metric to judge if satisfaction is static, increasing or decreasing. One common customer satisfaction metric is the net promoter score (NPS). The net promoter score is based on answers to one question: "how likely would you be to

recommend XYZ business to a friend or colleague?" Respondents are asked to give a ranking on a scale of 1-10. Those who rank a 9 or 10 are considered promoters. Those who rank a 7 or 8 are passive. Those who rank 6 or below are considered detractors. In the calculation of an NPS, the proportion of detractors are subtracted from the proportion of promoters — thus resulting in a net promoter score. NPS can also be used to gauge employee satisfaction.

Innovation

- How much money spent is spent annually on research and development?
- How many new products are released per year?
- What is the profitability of new products?
- How much time and money is spent on training and development of staff?
- How much time is allocated to ideation?

AUTHOR'S NOTE: *There are many qualitative measures that can help inform business decisions, and it is also possible to have too much data available. It can be overwhelming to sift through a long list of metrics. When choosing which non-financial measures to track, consider leading or lagging indicators in your business. Leading indicators are measurable factors that change at some point before the economic, financial, or business variable it is correlated with changes. Sales orders are an example of a leading indicator because it signals future revenue that has not yet been sold. Lagging indicators change at some point after the economic, financial, or business variable it is correlated with changes. Company profit is an example of a lagging indicator because it is measured and observed only after business operations have taken place.*

Thoughtful analysis can be used to shed light on almost all business problems. Understanding the "why" behind numerical data can point the way to a solution. Often the key to solving problems or making major decisions is having better data, sharper data, so options can be analyzed at a deep enough level that it spotlights changes that need to be made.

AUTHOR'S NOTE: *Key takeaway: The faster that a company grows, coupled with the volatility and/or pace of change of its industry, the more frequent that company should plan its strategy.*

Strategy doesn't have to be a week-long retreat with flowery ideals. It can be a few tweaks here and there to the existing plan. But the faster your world is moving, the more frequently you will need to gently correct course.

CHAPTER **SEVEN**

Budgeting

The budget is the essential financial roadmap to achieve company goals. When working with new clients, one of my first questions is "Do you have an annual budget process?" From my perspective, this is an indicator of financial acumen. A budget expresses guideposts in dollars so a company can see if it is on track to meet expectations. In this chapter, I'll break down the ways a budget can help a company manage its business as well as the pros and cons of different budget methodologies.

A STRATEGIC AND MANAGERIAL TOOL

The budget is a tool that creates alignment within the leadership team. Often, the budget process will follow a strategic planning session. While big picture goals are defined in the strategic planning session, the budget process metes out those ideas into defined financial targets. Big goals are crystallized into specific strategies for each department and financial metrics are assigned to each strategy.

In addition to clarifying company goals, the budget process is a gut check on whether the are achievable. Articulating goals is like creating an outline of the picture of the future, and the budgets that support that vision color in the lines — the picture of the future becomes much

Each department head should be responsible for writing own budget that aligns with company goals, and thus creates alignment within the team. Knowing that he or she will be held accountable to the budget, department heads generally have much more buy-in tha they would without going through the process.

BUDGET AS MANAGEMENT TOOL

Many people think of a budget as something that is a one-time event that happens in the fourth quarter, after which it goes in a drawer never to be reviewed again until next year. This approach leaves so much value on the table. A living budget can serve as a north star, keeping a company on track all year.

It can be used to drive accountability. In the monthly review of financials, the budget versus actual reports should be reviewed by department so that each department head is truly held accountable for his performance. Compensation structure should be tied to ability of the individual to manage the budget.

The cardinal rule of using budgeting to drive accountability is to hold people accountable only for factors within their control. To tie one's compensation to managing a metric for which he or she has no authority does not make sense. For example, a tasting room manager should not be held accountable for the actual versus budgeted spend on rent expense because it is unlikely that the tasting room manager will have the authority to negotiate a lease agreement.

My recommendation is to clearly define which accounts the key employee will be responsible for managing and include only those in the employee's evaluation.

EXPLAINING THE DIFFERENCES BETWEEN BUDGET VERSUS ACTUAL RESULTS

When reviewing financial results with your leaders, the purpose of highlighting cost overruns or underperforming revenue is not to punish department heads for being off the mark from what was budgeted; the purpose is to understand *why* actual results were different than what was anticipated. By getting to the heart of why results were different than the budget a team can hone in on the types of changes needed to move the organization towards the desired result. Another option is that a team may discover that the original forecast was unattainable, and expectations should be revised.

I recommend having department heads present their own department's results to the rest of the leadership team during the financial review. This encourages ownership of results.

Finally, take action. Once a company understands why a result is different than expected, it can change behavior in order to change future results.

DIFFERENT BUDGET METHODOLOGIES

There are multiple types of budgets, and three of the most common are the static budget, the flexible budget, and a rolling forecast.

The static budget is one set of numbers that stays the same throughout the year. Set it and forget it. This is the most basic version of a budget. A static budget is usually created in the fourth quarter of the preceding year. It is not updated during the year unless there are significant structural changes to the operation.

The flexible budget establishes a financial outcome dependent on the level of activity. In other words, the sales level dictates the budget. Cost of goods sold and expenses are categorized as either variable or fixed. Variable expenses change based on the level of activity (for example, raw materials cost) and fixed costs are static over a relevant range (for example, rent). A flexible budget will display a different financial outcome depending on how many units are assumed to be sold. In the example below, the middle column assumes sales of 100,000 proof gallons and the right column assumes sales of 80,000 proof gallons. As you scan down the columns, you see some rows change and some stay the same. The rows that change represent variable costs; the rows that stay the same represent fixed costs. *(Table 7.1)*

In Table 7.1, which is built in Excel, the cell containing "80,000" does not have a formula. Meaning, the user should hard-key in that quantity. In this example we assume that 80,000 was the actual level of production for the period. All other rows will adapt based on the input in that cell. With a flexible budget company leaders can clearly see what the budgeted result when using the actual units sold for the period. Creating a template like Table 7.1 allows the company to measure actual results against reasonable budgeted results based on a specific level of activity.

A flexible budget takes more work to set up than a standard budget because each line item needs to be coded based on whether it is fixed or variable. While the results of a flexible budget can be quite useful, it may not be logistically possible for all companies because it takes effort to set up.

Table 7.1

FLEXIBLE BUDGET EXAMPLE		
Sales in PG	100,000	80,000
Revenue	$ 5,000,000	$ 4,000,000
COGS	$ 2,400,000	$ 1,920,000
Gross Margin	$ 2,600,000	$ 2,080,000
Gross Margin %	52%	52%
Rent	$ 120,000	$ 120,000
Payroll, Taxes and Benefits	$ 530,000	$ 530,000
Sales and Marketing	$ 450,000	$ 360,000
Other Operating Expenses	$ 984,000	$ 984,000
Total Costs	$ 2,084,000	$ 1,994,000
EBITDA	$ 516,000	$ 86,000
Interest	$ 42,000	$ 42,000
Taxes	$ 20,640	$ 3,440
Depreciation	$ 40,000	$ 40,000
Amortization	$ 5,000	$ 5,000
Net Income	$ 408,360	$ (4,440)

Even if a company is working with a static budget, should analyze whether the actual performance is good or bad relative to the budget at the given level of sales. For example, as the world slowly emerges from the COVID-19 pandemic, perhaps restaurant revenue is down 20% from budget. In a review of performance, COGS may be considerably under budget (which would normally be celebrated), but the question is "Are the COGS under budget *enough* even when considering the decline in sales?" If restaurant sales are down 20% but restaurant COGS are down only 13%, then COGS are not being properly managed.

The rolling forecast is a variation of the budget process that takes the current month's performance and uses that information to inform the budget for the same month next year. (For instance, September 2022 actual results will be used to budget for September 2023.) This scenario requires budgeting one month at a time. The actual results for one month inform the budget for the same month next year. This is an ideal way to budget because it keeps the topic alive within the leadership team from month to month, and it reinforces the message that each department is accountable for results. I also believe this method yields a more accurate budget. And finally, it is more likely that changes or adaptations to process will happen in a timely manner. In sum, the rolling forecast is the best budget methodology for establishing budget management as part of the company's culture.

PROCESS FOR BUILDING A BUDGET

Rule #1: Sales set the tone. All other budgets flow from the sales projection.

In figure 7.1, the top half revenue centers and the bottom half expense centers. Create a separate budget for each item on the flow chart. These will be consolidated into one master budget by the CFO.

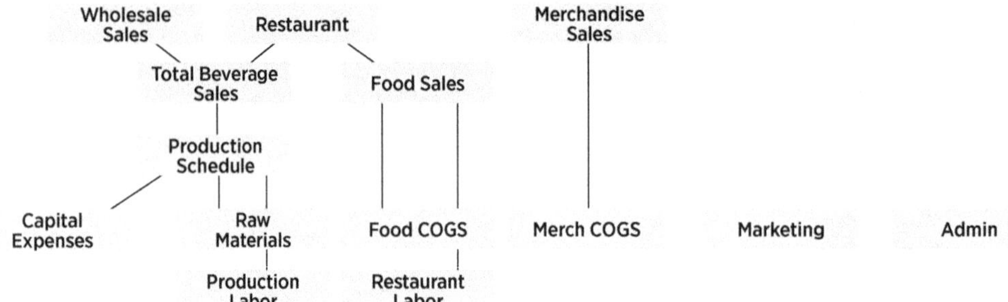

Figure 7.1

CREATING YOUR SALES BUDGET

Forecast your sales by case equivalents or proof gallons for the future year by distributor, by SKU, by month. Create an Excel workbook, and each distributor will have its own tab. (If you have a restaurant or tasting room, each location should be on its own tab.) Add a tab that lists the sales price per SKU by distributor. Finally, create a revenue roll-up tab in which the volume forecast to be sold is multiplied by the correct sales price for that item per distributor.

Once revenue is agreed upon, the Head Brewer or Production Manager can use this information to create a production schedule. Following the production schedule, a budget for raw materials, labor, and capex is built.

The restaurant or tasting room manager builds out the food sales budget, from which food COGS and restaurant labor are derived. The merchandise manager will build his or her own budget. If a company does not have a merchandise manager, the restaurant or tasting room manager should build merchandise into budget.

Budgeting for online sales revenue is a toss-up. I generally ask the marketing manager to forecast these sales. Because fulfillment of online sales often falls to the marketing department, the department head probably has a finger on the pulse of that revenue stream.

Although the majority of the budget process involves income statement accounts, there are balance-sheet considerations as well, primarily with capital expenses (capex). Generally, the CFO will solicit a list of equipment requests from each department and prepare the capex budget. The CFO also prepares the administrative budget.

After all subsidiary budgets are compiled, the result is a forecast income statement, balance sheet and cash flow statement for the coming year. These reports are also called pro forma financials.

Step-by-step instructions for building a budget

Broadly speaking, there are three parts of the budget-building process:

1. Create departmental budgets
2. Consolidate
3. Refine

Start by having your CFO create templates in Excel for your revenue center department heads to complete. This is usually your sales director and tasting room manager. Come to consensus on projected sales for the coming year and get approval for the sales forecast from your CEO. Then provide a template to your distiller or head of production to work on the production schedule, raw materials, and labor budgets.

Meanwhile, the tasting room manager and marketing manager compile their cost budgets. The sales director produces the cost budget for that department. The CFO works on an administrative budget and a capital expenses budget.

The capital expense budget will be compiled based on information from department heads. The CFO should work with department heads to determine the fixed assets that are requested for the coming year.

AUTHOR'S NOTE:
CAPITAL PROJECT VETTING PROCESS
Companies should define the minimum investment amount for which capital projects must be vetted. For example, a company policy may state that projects over $10,000 must be analyzed and approved by the CFO, and projects over $200,000 must follow the same process as well as be approved by the Board of Directors.

When vetting a capital expense determine if financing is needed or if it can be paid out of cash flow. Present three financing options and discounted cash flow analysis for each option. Provide pro forma financial reports to show how the investment will affect the company.

All of these budgets are compiled, and the leadership team will have its first opportunity to see if the projected results when each department's input is combined. This is usually done in a team meeting. The intent of the meeting is to pressure test the assumptions of each department. Are sales projections so great that you cannot fulfill them in your current footprint? Will cash flow support the desired capex spends? Department heads should consider alternatives to solve any problem areas and refine their budget. Revised budgets are given to the CFO, who compiles them and redistributes for another round of conversation. After two to three rounds of revision, the company has worked out major issues and is left with a reasonable budget. *(Table 7.2)*

Table 7.2

Role	Responsibility
CFO	Compiles final budget, admin budget, capital expense budget, project manages the process
Sales Director	Wholesale sales budget
Tasting Room Manager	Sales budget for restaurants/tasting room, merchandise budget
Distiller	Production budget
Marketing Director	Marketing budget
CEO	Provides direction, approves final budget, holds department heads accountable for results

BUDGET CALENDAR

Table 7.3 is a suggested timeline for the standard budget process. Expect the process to take two to three months.

BUDGETING DISTILLERY RAW MATERIALS

Budgeting for raw materials is quite straightforward once the sales forecast is finalized.

If using a production planning software, export a report for the average COGS per proof gallon per brand of spirit produced in the prior year. Then use this average historical unit cost and multiply by the quantity of brand forecasted to be sold each month. Be sure to account for changes to raw materials costs resulting from a change in packaging materials, choice of vendors, change to bulk discounts, cost increases due to inflation, etc.

Step-by-step instructions for building a raw materials budget:

1. Generate a COGS by Brand report for all SKUs based on data from the last twelve months.
2. Create a Distillery COGS spreadsheet.
   a. One tab lists each brand on rows and COGS per proof gallon (or case equivalent) in a column.
   b. A second tab should be a copy of the sales forecast rollup (in proof gallons or cash equivalents) by month from the Sales Budget.
   c. The third tab will be the product of COGS per proof gallon times the quantity budgeted to be sold of each brand. (In other words, the COGS per proof gallon will be multiplied by the quantity to be sold). The total from the third tab is the budgeted raw materials COGS for wholesale sales.

Table 7.3

Date	Responsible Party	Activity
9/20/20XX	CFO, CEO, Department Heads (Tasting Room Manager, Director of Sales, Distiller, Director of Marketing)	CFO delivers budget worksheets to department heads
9/27/20XX	Department Heads	Initial budgets delivered to CFO
10/4/20XX	CFO	Initial budgets are consolidated and delivered to leadership team
10/11/20XX	CFO, CEO, Department Heads	Budget work session with leadership team
10/18/20XX	CFO	Distribute updated budgets with notes from work session
10/25/20XX	Department Heads	Second round of budgets due from department heads
11/8/20XX	CFO	Consolidate second round of budget and deliver to leadership team.
11/22/20XX	CFO, CEO, Department Heads	Final leadership team work session.
11/25/20XX	CEO	Sign off on final budget.
11/30/20XX	CFO	Final consolidated and departmental budgets issued

ESTABLISHING A TEMPLATE FOR A TASTING ROOM

The budget template for a restaurant or tasting room often starts with assigning costs as fixed or variable, and then forming assumptions on how those costs will increase or decrease based on historical data. The budget template should be formula driven so that the tasting room manager is filling in cells related to how a line item will increase or decrease.

Step-by-step instructions for building a tasting room budget:

1. Generate the income statement for the tasting room by month for the last 24 months (if you don't have two years of data, include as many prior periods as possible). Export to Excel.
2. Add columns for the budgeted year's months.
3. Add key percentages:
    a. Add a column to the right of the COGS dollars for COGS percentage relative to that category's revenue.
    b. Add a row under gross margin dollars for gross margin percentage of revenue.
    c. Add a row under key subtotals for year-over-year change, expressed in as a percentage.
4. Add a column to the left and assign each COGS and Expense account as Fixed or Variable
5. Add a second tab for assumptions for the budgeted year. Copy all COGS and Expense accounts into Column A.
    a. In column B, the restaurant or tasting room manager should add the percentage by which he or she believes this cost will increase or decrease.
    b. Column C allows the manager to provide any details not captured elsewhere in the model, but which may be relevant.
6. The first tab should be formatted so that forecast year expenses are derived from historical data and assumptions for the coming year. For example, if tasting-room labor is expected to follow the same trends annually and also increase 5%, the formula for the January forecast tasting-room labor would be an average of January from the two prior years' data times the 5% increase from the second tab.

PULLING IT ALL TOGETHER

After departmental budgets are created, the CFO will consolidate them all into one master budget. Every department budgeted income statement will be a separate tab in the same Excel workbook. Create one summary income statement that combines data from the departmental tabs. Once the consolidated income statement is created, a Balance Sheet and Statement of Cash Flows can be forecast.

Seeing all data accumulated into a set of financial reports will reveal areas that need to be adjusted. Should capex be added to achieve the sales goals? Are there months where cash is falling too low? Can bank covenants be met every quarter?

Answering these questions and developing solutions to problem areas will require the leadership team to work together. After a few rounds of revision, the result is an intentional roadmap that leads the company closer to its goals.

FROM BUDGET TO FORECAST

"Skate to where the puck is going to be, not where it has been." — Wayne Gretzky

A review of budget vs actual reports is a comparison of current performance in the current situation to current performance in an old situation. Measuring performance to budget means that the leadership anchors its expectations to the past — they are looking in the rearview mirror, whereas creating a rolling forecast allows leadership to scan the horizon, move to the future. "Skating to where the puck is going to be," so to speak. To embrace a rolling forecast as a management tool a company will need to commit to more maintenance of the document. The forecast is updated each month as actual results become known and better information is available in order to predict expectations for the remainder of the year.

A budget is a plan made with the best information available at the time it is created, which is usually in the fourth quarter of the preceding year. There is no flexibility to adjust for unforeseen changes. Examples of what might change: a global pandemic, distributor consolidations, change in consumer preferences, packaging material shortages.

A budget is a plan for a static set of circumstances. Current performance is measured against expectations that were set in the past. A forecast is a plan for a flexible scenario. Current performance is measured against the most recent actual results.

CREATING A FORECAST MODEL

A forecast doesn't replace the need for a budget. A budget serves as the starting point for a forecast. Updating a forecast on a monthly basis keeps management attuned to the rhythms of the business and predicting what will happen becomes a much less mysterious endeavor. There is no need to reforecast the entire budget each month; high-level forecasts are just as effective, for example, forecasting only big-ticket items like Revenue, COGS, Labor, and Operating Expenses. If a category appears to be out of reasonable range, then management should dive into the detail to gain clarity. Consider the level of detail that needs to be updated each period. If management is spending more time, money and resources updating the forecast model than the benefit the model gives to company, a simpler tool should be chosen! It's a cost-benefit analysis.

Table 7.4 shows two months of actual data and three months of forecast. This is a condensed example, and in reality the forecast portion would go out for 12 months. Note that this model combines the Income Statement with elements of the Balance Sheet, so in one report, the effect on cash can be seen. This is not a standard financial report, but rather a report created

Table 7.4

		Actual		Forecast	
	Month 1	Month 2	Month 3	Month 4	Month 5
Revenue	$100,000	$110,000	$105,000	$120,000	$130,000
COGS	$6,000	$63,800	$45,150	$49,200	$52,000
Gross Margin	**$40,000**	**$46,200**	**$59,850**	**$70,800**	**$78,000**
GM%	**40%**	**42%**	**43%**	**41%**	**40%**
OpEx					
Labor	$15,000	$15,000	$15,450	$15,450	$15,600
Sales/Mktg	$1,500	$1,500	$1,600	$1,600	$1,500
Facilities	$5,000	$5,000	$5,000	$5,000	$5,000
Other	$7,500	$7,500	$7,200	$8,000	$7,500
Total OpEx	$29,000	$29,000	$29,250	$30,050	$29,600
Net Operating Income	**$11,000**	**$17,200**	**$30,600**	**$40,750**	**$48,400**
NOI%	11%	16%	29%	34%	37%
Change in A/R	$ (15,000)	$10,000	$ (7,500)	$ (5,000)	$ (12,500)
Change in A/P	$ (5,000)	$5,000	$5,000	$5,000	$5,000
Change in Inventory	$2,000	$ (3,000)	$ (1,000)	$2,000	$ (500)
Change in other balance sheet items	$ (50)	$80	$ (50)	$40	$120
Change in Debt	$15,000	$ (30,000)	$ (5,000)	$ (5,000)	$ (5,000)
Change in Equity	$ (5,000)				
Total Change in Cash	**$2,950**	**$ (720)**	**$22,050**	**$37,790**	**$35,520**
Beginning of Period Cash	**$25,000**	**$27,950**	**$27,230**	**$49,280**	**$87,070**
End of Period Cash	**$27,950**	**$27,230**	**$49,280**	**$87,070**	**$122,590**

for management purposes.

Of all rows in the chart, end-of-period cash is most important. Keep your eye on ending cash and be aware of months that are predicted to be dangerously low. Net operating income is the second most important number on the model. (Remember, cash is king!)

Below net operating income is a section that shows the change in balance sheet accounts (beginning of period balance versus end of period balance). Changes to balance sheet accounts affect cash flow and therefore must be included in order to have a reasonable forecast cash balance.

Two accounts that are particularly challenging to forecast are Accounts Receivable and Accounts Payable. To forecast change in AR, tie your projected AR to your DSO (Days Sales Outstanding) metric. If you average 20 days sales outstanding, then assume that the AR balance will equal the previous 20 days' sales. To forecast change in AP, tie your projected balance to a % of your COGS and operating expenses (excluding labor) for the month. For example, to project the forecast AP at the end of April, review the average data for April in the previous year or two. Calculate Accounts Payable/(COGS + operating expenses) for those historical periods and, assuming no major changes to the business structure have happened since those historical months, apply that percentage to the forecast April AP.

RHYTHM OF FORECAST UPDATES

The first step of generating a forecast is to create an annual budget by month in the fourth quarter of the year prior to the budget period. At the close of the first month, replace the forecast Month 1 with the actual Month 1 results. Given the actual results of Month 1, consider what changes should be made to future months through end of year. Keep any changes high level. Factors to consider are revenue, sales mix, COGS %, operating expenses for broad categories (such as labor, sales and marketing, and facilities). Monthly updates help you see what you have done year-to-date and where you expect to end the year. Keeping the forecast at a high level makes it easy and quick to update.

Some key metrics to consider: average profit per case, breakeven revenue, number of weeks of cash on hand, A/R days sales outstanding, and inventory turnover. The metrics that you choose to measure should be useful to *your* company. It's more meaningful to assess the *movement* of a metric than it is to assess its absolute value.

USING A FORECAST AS A MANAGEMENT TOOL

Review your forecast monthly with the leadership team. Ask department heads to provide assumptions for the forecast periods. The monthly review allows the organization to consider if assumptions are reasonable. For example, if your head of Sales estimates that case sales will double next month, your head of Production may take issue with that estimate. He may understand that the facility doesn't have the time or capacity to fulfill double the quantity on order. The monthly review with the leadership team helps department heads gain a better understanding of the organization's finances. It forces them to think proactively about what they know will happen in the coming months and how that will affect revenues and expenses. The forecast allows the financial planning aspect of the organization to be a living, breathing activity, not something that happens once per year.

Use your forecast to answer questions like "Are we profitable?" "How close are our sales to our targets?" "Where are we spending money?" "Is our operation self-sustainable?" The sooner your team sees changes happening in the financials, the faster they can respond. Timely response minimizes the risk of a multiple-month decline.

Real-Life Application

I started working at a mobile canning and bottling company in 2014 in an entry level position. I worked my way up to management and eventually to Operations Manager. In 2019 the company sold to a distillery. When the company was acquired, I moved into the distillery side of the business. First, I served as Production Manager and after a period of time in that role was promoted to Director of Operations.

At the distillery I helped implement the sales and operations forecast. We used the forecast to determine if we had enough raw materials on hand to meet our sales targets, and we used it to ensure that production was planned to allow us to meet sales targets. We would review this monthly. We looked twelve months into the future, by month by SKU. We also broke down the data to look at the projected performance of each different sales region. The forecast was never "done"; we used it as a working document and continuously tweaked our future actions based on the data in the plan. By mid-year we had seen the forecast dozens of times and it was changing in small ways each time. If we brought a new products to market we would integrate that into the model. If we became aware of new market research we would add that in. If compliance changed in one of the states where we sold product, we would make sure any sales or production effects were captured in the forecast. We also did co-packing for a period of time, and that introduced a whole other level of planning and compliance.

Our forecast affected more than just sales and production. It also affected the to-do list of our compliance, which feel under my area of responsibility. I was the point person for label and formula approvals and was the liaison with our outsourced partner who prepared excise tax returns and other state compliance.

We were a big operation but didn't use fancy software. Our forecasts were done in Excel. The forecast always started with sales — per SKU, per month, per region. This would then go to operations, and as I mentioned, we were very frequently updating the model for small changes here and there. We had a financial analyst on staff who was an incredible asset to the organization, and who helped us make these updates in a timely manner.

As Director of Operations, most of my interaction with finance was related to my obligation to manage to a budget. I was given guidelines within which I was told to work and was expected to keep costs as low as possible. I think my biggest interaction with the finance team was working on the COGS budget. I was providing perspective about how to minimize COGS from a boots-on-the-ground perspective. We included in COGS direct materials, production overhead, labor, and management overhead.

Our finance team built our

cost accounting spreadsheet and I provided input on the cost of different components: bottles, the juice inside (which of course varied depending on age of the spirit and its proof gallon), the cork or capsule components, etc. I was often brought in to determine what was logistically possible. For example, if we wanted to swap out a closure on a bottle, I would be asked to assess if this could be done and how it would affect operations. One of my more detailed projects was to create a calculation of the water that needed to be added per SKU to achieve the desired proof gallon per bottle. That information coupled with our water bill gave us enough information to back into an accurate COGS for water used in the process of each SKU.

Our company focused on high margin, low volume products. The marketing strategy positioned our products as scarce in the marketplace. We were demand driven. The goal was to hit 60% to 70% margin on each SKU. The average bottle shelf price was $75, and high-end single malt products were priced to the consumer around $150. Our low-end was, maybe, $60. The company really targeted a specific market.

To meet those aggressive margins, we watched COGS very closely. I worked with the finance team to provide up-to-date costing information so that we could maintain COGS benchmarks as much as possible. This included working with production to make sure the physical production costs were as low as possible or working to build a new standard operating procedures to reduce the touches needed. We always were aware of how lean we could make our operations.

A lot of my work was in Six Sigma and lean manufacturing. We wanted to maintain a tight production flow. We targeted 30% of sales mix on higher volume products, 70% of sales mix on low volume high margin products. High volume products were produced at a rate 2,000 cases per week; lower volume products were produced at a rate of 200-300 cases per year.

To wrap up, I'll leave you with one piece of advice: buy once, cry once. Do not ever skimp on any piece of production equipment. Always buy the top of the line and go at least 60% larger than you ever think you are going to need. Worst case scenario, you can always run a smaller production quantity. I really believe in having quality stainless and packaging lines. Look, you can buy a cheap drill that will last two jobs; or you can buy a nice drill that will last forever and has a great warranty. Go for the quality product. The same is true for software! Don't get a subpar software system. We outgrew our system the day that we got it. The finance team and the C-suite didn't want to take the time to onboard a new software, and so we were stuck with a band-aid solution. Go for the best — buy once, cry once.

Jonathan, anonymous

CHAPTER **EIGHT**

Key Performance Indicators

Whereas the financials are a full report of a business's health, key performance indicators (KPIs) are like the executive summary. KPIs often provide information from various financial reports or even nonfinancial data and present it as one number. KPIs are a shortcut to many common business questions

It's not necessary to pore over full financials every week (although these reviews should be done at least monthly). Instead, honing in on a few key numbers will allow a manager to stay up to date on performance.

KPIs can measure almost any area of business health. Some common areas tracked are liquidity, sales and profitability. Liquidity is a company's ability to pay obligations as they come due. It relates to cash and current assets vs current liabilities. It answers questions such as "Do we have a sufficient safety net of cash? Are we at risk of being unable to pay our bills?" Sales measures your growth rate. It is a focus on the top line of the business. Profitability answers the question "Are we making money?" This is indicated by gross margin (revenue - cost of goods sold) and net income (revenue - all expenses).

LIQUIDITY RATIOS

Current Ratio

The current ratio is calculated as current assets/ current liabilities. The ratio measures liquidity. It speaks to an organization's ability to pay obligations as they come due. The target ratio is 2:1. *(Table 8.1, next page)*

Quick Ratio

The quick ratio is calculated as (current assets-inventory) / current liabilities. This ratio is an even stricter measure of liquidity. It restricts the numerator to cash and near-cash assets. The target ratio is 1.5:1. This target is lower if aged spirits is a large component of inventory.

Table 8.1

Ratio	Formula	What it means
Current Ratio	Current Assets / Current Liabilities	Measures how well a company is positioned to pay its obiligations as they come due.
Quick Ratio	(Current Assets – Inventory) / Current Liabilities	Measures how well a company is able to pay its obligations when due. Higher ratio = more financially secure in the short term.
Working Capital	Current Assets / Current Liabilities	Measures efficiency and short-term financial health.
Debt to Equity	Total Liabilities / Total Equity	Measures financial leverage and indicates how much debt a company is using to finance assets relative to equity.
Days Cash Available	Cash / (Annual Operating Budget/365)	Measures how long the organization can pay operating expenses without receiving additional cash.

TABLE 8.2 Sample Monthly Balance Sheet

As of December 31, 2019

ASSETS	
Current Assets	
Checking/Savings	188,568.86
Accounts Receivable	280,300.96
Other Current Assets	232,620.57
Total Current Assets	701,490.39
Fixed Assets	92,461.47
Other Assets	380,771.76
TOTAL ASSETS	**1,174,723.62**
LIABILITIES & EQUITY	
Liabilities	
Current Liabilitites	
Accounts Payable	195,233.28
Credit Cards	10,780.15
Other Current Liabilities	536,722.04
Total Current Liabilities	742,735.47
Long Term Liabilities	368,831.27
Total Liabilities	1,111,566.74
Equity	63,156.88
TOTAL LIABILITIES & EQUITY	**1,174,723.62**

Current Ratio:

$701,490.39/$742,735.47 = .94

Quick Ratio:

($188,568.86 + 280,300.96) /

$742,735.47 = .63

Debt to Equity:

$1,111,566.74 / $63,156.88 = 17.6

Working capital

Working capital is a measure of the resources available to run the operations of the company.

Debt to Equity

Debt to equity is measured by dividing total liabilities by total equity.

This ratio measures the degree to which a company is leveraged. Simply speaking, leverage means that a company is in debt. It is the use of debt to maximize profits returned to equity holders. To finance an operation, a company may choose debt or equity. Debt means the company has borrowed money; equity means the owners have financed it themselves. Aggressive leveraging practices are often associated with high levels of risk. This condition may result in volatile earnings as a result of the additional interest expense and can limit the ability to borrow money, thus reducing financial flexibility.

Days Cash Available

This metric measures the number of days that an organization can pay its operating expenses with the amount of cash currently on hand.

For the current ratio, quick ratio, and working capital, a higher ratio is better. For debt to equity, a lower ratio is better. For days cash available, more days are better (up to a point).

Cash Position

Cash is the oxygen of any business. The more cash available, the greater the financially flexibility. What is included in cash position? Cash, credit card receivables, certificates of deposit, and other highly liquid instruments.

A company's cash position signals financial health. The cash balance serves as a buffer to guard against losses and a reserve from which to make investments. Having too much cash on hand indicates that assets are underutilized. The opportunity cost (i.e., potential returns a business is missing out on by keeping cash in the bank) is called "cash drag." When viewed as an investment vehicle, cash that sits dormant has a negative return due to inflation. *(Table 8.3)*

SALES RATIOS

Inventory Turnover

Inventory Turnover shows how many times a company's inventory is sold and replaced over a period of time. A low turnover implies excess inventory and/or room to improve sales. A high ratio implies either strong sales and/or large discounts.

Asset turnover

Asset turnover measures the value of a company's sales or revenues generated relative to the value of its assets. A higher number is better.

Days sales inventory

Days sales inventory measures how many days of sales a company could fill with the current inventory level. It is calculated as average inventory / COGS * 365. A lower calculation is preferred, and I recommend

Table 8.3

Ratio	Formula	What it means	Target
Inventory Turnover	Cost of Goods Sold / Inventory	Measures how fast a company sells inventory and is generally compared against industry averages	2
Asset Turnover	Revenue / Total Assets	Indicates the efficiency with which a company is deploying its assets in generating revenue	1 — 1.5
Gross Margin Percentage	(Revenue - Cost of Goods Sold) / Revenue	Measures the percentage of sales price that is available to cover operating expenses	50% - 54%

tying the target to forecast sales, although this becomes less strongly correlated if aged spirits is a substantial part of inventory. Other sales measurements include:

- Shipments — sales of product from a producer's warehouse to a wholesaler and/ or retailer.
- Depletions — sales from a retailer to an end consumer
- Shipments vs depletions
- Points of distribution — locations where product can be purchased. A bar, restaurant, state-controlled liquor store, and big box retailer are all examples of points of distribution.
- Velocity — the rate of sale of a particular SKU from a retailer's point of distribution.

PROFITABILITY RATIOS

Gross margin is a KPI that should be tracked in aggregate, by sales channel (eg, retail vs wholesale), and by SKU. *(Table 8.4)*

Example: one 750mL bottle of vodka

Sales price	**$15**	**100%**
Labor and materials	**$5**	**33.3%**
Excise Tax	**$2.14**	**14.3%**
Total cost	**$7.14**	**47.6%**
Gross margin	**$7.86**	**52.4%**

Net operating income

Net operating income can also be expressed as a dollar amount or a percentage. Net income in dollars is calculated as Gross Margin — Operating Expenses; as a percentage, it is calculated as (Gross Margin - Operating Expenses)/Revenue. The metric measures how much a company is making from operations.

Net income

Net income can be expressed as a dollar amount or a percentage. Net income in dollars is calculated as Operating Income +/- Other Income/Expense; as a percentage, it is calculated as (Operating Income +/- Other Income/Expense)/Revenue. This figure answers the question "What is our bottom line?"

EBITDA

EBITDA is a metric that allows a reasonable comparison between companies that may have been financed differently, or have different depreciation policies. EBITDA is commonly used by investors and analysts to measure the value of a company.

PRODUCTION MEASURES

The following metrics focus on the production operations and the efficiency of the production process.

- Packaging labor efficiencies
  - Cost of packaged goods sold/packaging labor expense
- Production labor efficiencies
  - Cost of goods sold / production labor expense
- Revenue per labor dollar
  - Revenue / labor expense
- Percentage of capacity
  - Production in proof gallons / production capacity in proof gallons

Table 8.4

Ratio	Formula	What it means	Target
EBITDA	Net Income + Interest + Taxes + Depreciation + Amortization	Common measure of the earning potential of the business. Often used by investors to compare companies.	10%-14%
Return on Assets	Net Income / Total Assets	Indicates the efficiency with which a company is deploying its assets in generating revenue. A higher result is desired.	Depends on factors in EBITDA
Return on Equity	Net Income / Shareholders Equity	Measures how much profit a company generates with the money shareholders have invested	Depends on factors in EBITDA

LABOR EFFICIENCY

Labor is usually the largest expense in any organization. Labor efficiency measures how much profit is generated by each dollar of labor. As long as labor efficiency ratio is meeting the defined range of success, a company will keep growing.

To obtain the most actionable data, each type of labor must be measured differently. There are likely separate groups of employees involved in production, sales and admin. Production labor is a cost of goods sold, so percentage of revenue is the most appropriate measure of production labor. A recommended efficiency ratio for production labor is $20 — that is, $20 of revenue for every $1 of production labor.

Alternatively, sales and admin labor are considered operating expenses and are not included in COGS. These labor costs should be measured against contribution margin. Contribution margin is revenue minus variable costs. A recommended efficiency ratio for sales labor is $7 -- $7 of contribution margin for each $1 of labor, and for admin labor is $5 -- $5 of contribution margin for each $1 of administrative labor.

As you see, there are many choices when it comes to metrics for measuring business health. Don't feel that you need to track them all — indeed, that would be overwhelming. Choose one or two from each area to track on a regular basis.

The presentation of KPIs and ratios can take many formats. They can be simple Excel charts, or more sophisticated visuals. Here are a few ideas of how a business may want to look at its metrics.

Example A, Figure 8.1 is from a business analytics software. Clearly, the presentation is not something that can be whipped up in Excel. Many business intelligence softwares are available that analyze financial data and present it in a visual manner. A visual presentation can be very helpful because it allows the presenter to communicate complex information in a simple, relatable format – easy to understand even if someone doesn't understand accounting.

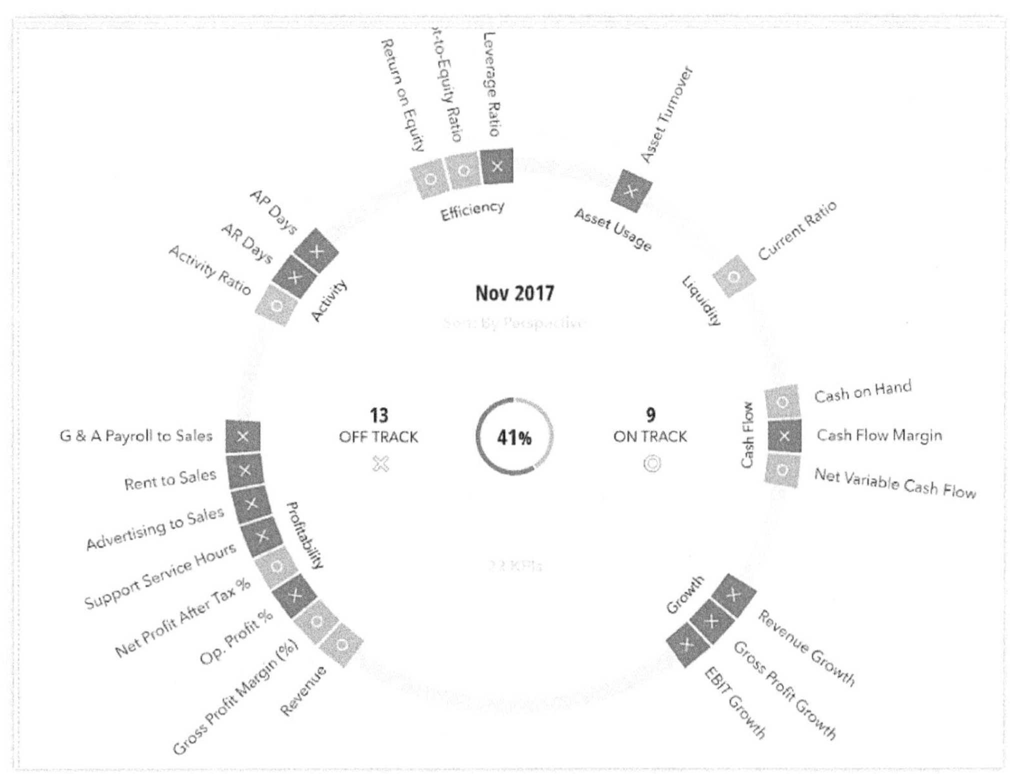

Figure 8.1

Example B, Figure 8.2 is more straightforward and presented as a chart. This presentation could be built in Excel. Choose a presentation that is easy to prepare and understandable to your audience. The form it takes does not matter; it does matter that it is reviewed frequently!

Once a KPI dashboard is built, the pulse of a company can be seen at a quick glance. Investing in someone who can update the data in an accurate, timely manner will make the information even more useful. This information should be shared with the leadership team. Break out KPIs by department and hold department leaders accountable for their results Additionally, share KPI results with other organizational stakeholders like lenders and investors.

KPIs help business owners stay attuned to the performance of their company. Identifying the key performance indicators requires management to identify what success means to them. Success is not defined the same way for every organization, and therefore the KPIs a company chooses to measure should be meaningful to the specific business. Understanding the drivers of each key performance indicator allows management to focus on the input that needs to be adjusted to effect the desired outcome. Consistent review of key indicators gives a quick assessment of what's working, what's not, and where energy should be focused to create change.

	1 ALERT	RESULT	TARGET		TREND	IMPORTANCE
A PROFITABILITY		NOV 2017			vs OCT 2017	
Total Revenue		$352,298	$10,000	✓	▼ -7.1%	Critical
Gross Profit Margin (%)		98%	30%	✓	▲ 8%	Medium
Operating Profit Margin		18.01%	25%	✕	▼ -0.5%	High
Net Profit After Tax Margin		17.86%	7%	✓	▼ -1.94%	Medium
Support Service Hours		$108,604	$900,000	✕	▼ -28.5%	Low
Advertising to Sales		0.05%	0%	✕	▼ -0.01%	Low
Rent to Sales		2.14%	0%	✕	▲ 0.11%	Low
G & A Payroll to Sales		1.89%	0%	✕	▲ 0.16%	Low
B ACTIVITY						
Activity Ratio		3.71 times	2.00 times	✓	▼ -0.34 times	Critical
Accounts Receivable Days		44.00 days	40.00 days	✕	▲ 4.00 days	Medium
Accounts Payable Days	●	-1.00 days	45.00 days	✕	▼ -1.00 days	Medium
C EFFICIENCY						
Return on Equity		77.04%	15%	✓	▼ -19.2%	Critical
Debt-to-Equity Ratio		0.50	0.00	✓	▼ -0.04	Low
Debt Leverage Ratio		0.33	0.00	✕	▼ -0.02	Low

Figure 8.2

Real-Life Application

I started our business when I was in college at Portland State University. I was studying business management and finance and was planning on continuing my studies into intellectual property and corporate law. Things took a turn, though. During my time at PSU one of the hobbies I picked up was distilling craft spirits. That was in the days where you saw a new brewery popping up on every block and distilleries started doing that, too. Distillery Row in Portland was starting to become a thing. It was fascinating to me that you could create a unique spirit by adding ingredients to infuse it. I was also at an age where I couldn't buy spirits, but I could make them! My friend, who later became my business partner, and I were playing around with different infusions. Neither of us came from a science, fermentation, or chemistry background - we were business students - so we didn't know that you could make a flavored vodka using additives, chemicals, or extracts. We thought you would just use real fruit. That was at the time when all of these crazy flavored vodkas were flooding the market. Fortunately, we actually found a hole in the market which was a real fruit infused vodka using no additives. It was innovative at the time. Now you're seeing more people using real fruit or essences and trying to go natural, but the better-for-you category wasn't a thing when we were launching the brand.

Also, the law had recently changed in Oregon to allow samplings and tastings and sell at farmers markets and events. We used that to our advantage. We went to farmers markets, berry festivals, went to conventions. We even went to gun shows, hunting shows, and boat shows. We did just about everything. We believed in our product, we just had to get people to try it. We grew the brand that way.

Being in the industry and seeing the products that were out there, I became inspired to create more. I wanted to get into different categories, different price points, and different consumers. That's when we created Cascade Spirits. Cascade Spirits is a house of brands. We have whiskey, gin, a well program. We really take it market by market, understand the customers, and provide them a product that's superior, whether that's price point, availability, or just the juice itself. Under Cascade Spirits we have four brands that we produce internally and one other that we manage - a total of five.

We launched Wild Roots, our vodka line, in July 2013. We launched with a raspberry vodka and four months later, in November, we launched a marionberry vodka. It took a year before we launched another flavor, and that was apple cinnamon; we launched that in the fall of 2014. Innovation really started to kick off in 2015 and 2016. We added cherry, huckleberry, pear, peach, cranberry. We added more SKUs but it wasn't until 2020 that we added more brands outside of Wild Roots. We really went deep with the first brand and then saw opportunity to capitalize on our infrastructure with the sales, finance, and operations team that we had. It allowed us to grow those brands without having as much expense. We acquired Broken Top whiskey and Cascade Potato vodka in early 2020 and we launched Sun Ranch spirits in August 2020.

I'm often asked about our considerations before launching a new product or flavor. There are a lot of different factors in the decision to put a new product in the market. I first start by reviewing our brand guidelines. Our brand is a fruit infused vodka inspired by the northwest. We're not the type of brand to launch a guava, mango, or coconut brand. We want fruit flavors that grow in our back yard and that we have access to. We explored the raspberry, marionberry, etc because those grow in our back yard. We don't use artificial flavors in our products; we let the fruit do the work for us, and it makes our job really easy.

In the production process some fruit comes out more than others, so there are practical considerations, too. For example, it's really hard to get a blueberry to look and taste the way you want it to. A blueberry will turn gray, and a strawberry will turn brown. If you think about it as a consumer, are they going to want a gray blueberry or a brown strawberry? I don't think so. Look, taste, feel, how it holds up over time are all factors. As are accessibility, pricing, and scalability. We knew that marionberries can only be sourced in this part of the country and that's going to be interesting this year. Because of the late freeze and late heat this season, the crops were diminished. In previous years our fruit cost about $70 per gallon. This year it's going to be over $300 per gallon. Over 90% of the marionberry crops were destroyed. We are looking at ways to work around these constraints, such as using a blackberry/marionberry blend. It would be doable because both fruits are in the same family, the color is similar, taste profile and feel are all very close. It's stepping outside our comfort zone, but it's still keeping product on the shelf and guaranteeing a good quality product.

When we look at product itself, it has to be about the taste first, then the packaging. Then we look at the competitive landscape. What's out there? How are they priced? Where do we need to be? Then we go to the financial projections. I like to say, "if it doesn't make dollars, it doesn't make sense". We were looking at a prickly pear flavor as a specialty item in Arizona, but it's too expensive. So if it doesn't meet our profitability thresholds, we don't produce it. It all goes back to the margins because we we need to make sure our margins are healthy enough to fund our growth.

To test a product, we do a research and development test batch to get the product right. Then we look at the financial data from the small production run and extrapolate it to scale. Then the scaled up financials are compared against our required minimum thresholds. I take it a step further and run it through our pricing program model, which shows the profitably of a product at regular price versus at a sale price. I always launch a product at regular price. That way, if there's some error and it costs more than we calculated, we can adjust and go up a few dollars on the shelf versus going down. From the consumer's perception it looks as if we launched at a promotional price, and the regular price is a few dollars higher.

I always try to shoot for high margins. Especially as relates to excise tax. You want to price your product for growth so that when you do go over that 100,000 proof gallon mark, and excise tax is higher, you aren't scrambling to cut costs in other areas in order to remain profitable.

When we were looking at launching new flavors, I decided to let the market be the ultimate arbiter of which ones would be widely distributed. We have eleven flavors in the Wild Roots brand, and all eleven are distributed in Oregon — our home state. Most other states only have five. We take the core products and the ones we see as best sellers and launch those in new states as we expand.

A varied portfolio also gives us this sense of stable overall margins. There's going to be seasons and times where raspberries and marionberries go up in cost, but apples, cherries and pears go down. And that gives us the ability to maintain a certain level of profitability as a company overall, even though a single product's profitability may fluctuate through the year. That was the other concept behind launching many flavors.

When we consider a new flavor and where to launch it, we think about the flavor. For example, if we were to launch a coconut vodka, we would first look at where coconut vodka sells and who the buyers are. Then I would try to build a marketing campaign that surrounds those buyers, but I wouldn't bring it to a mountain resort. That isn't to say that I would launch a coconut vodka only in a market where coconut grows natively. We really look at where it *sells*.

Research is at the heart of almost all of our decisions. We rely on it at the front end of the process when launching a product. On the financial front, I focus on margins. I like to look at margins by brand, by region, by package size. My dashboard is breaking it down to where I can get granular. Where are we making a lot of margin? Can we allocate marketing dollars to bring up margin in a particular sector? What are my investment states? Texas is not going to be a profitable state for us for a few years, because we have to invest in it first. We have to win in Texas. Whereas in Oregon, we are going to be very profitable. So if I see margins going down in states where we need to win, that's where I'll make some adjustments. I also look at the cost per sale and making sure that my sales and marketing spends are staying within the budget. I look at it as if I give my marketing team 7% to spend and I try to throttle my sales team. I always want to be profitable because I don't want to have to raise money. Raising money isn't fun! I look at the dollar amount of the cost of sale. That's is a quick way for me to determine if we are going to be profitable or not. The sales team can also tell quickly whether an investment makes sense. It forces them to know see their spends in terms of breakevens. What quantity do I have to sell to make this sales investment a good decision?

I also look at revenue per production labor. That's because there's a point where we need to expand. Does that mean employing a copacker, or do I need to think about building a production facility? I do try to look at numbers that will impact our company three to five years out.

For budgeting, I try to make future forecasts as detailed as possible. It's based on what we do now, but influenced by future decisions. One thing I'm looking at now is how efficient are we when people call in sick. What are the reasons why people are calling in sick? What are the motivators? Is it lack of benefits, or do they want more pay, or company perks? We talk to employees consistently. We've found that it's a week by week thing. I've changed our KPIs dramatically during COVID. That's switched form how many bottles are we producing every hour, to identifying the one thing to do is give me your best effort every day. Giving your best every day can create a culture of winning and our numbers are starting to turn in the right way. We check in with employees weekly. And the one thing we have noticed recetyl is that offering breakfast will really keep people engaged. It shows we care. And that matters to our employee. We ask employees what their aspirations are in 3 years, 5 years. Putting those data points around intangible aspects has been incredibly helpful data.

Our budgets are based off of sales. We have our sales forecasted by end of October. Then once I sign off on the revenue budget, the majority of the budget is done. From there we look at how the sales and marketing dollars are allocated. How much are we spending on different marketing outlets? I look at budget vs actual every month. And we aren't afraid to pivot if the numbers tell you to do so. Sometimes it's a shift in labor budget, sometimes it's marketing shift.

At the end of the day, my words of wisdom are: grow deep versus wide. It can be exciting to grow wide, ad it's flattering, but it's also very expensive. If you aren't financially prepared for that, it can be painful. Grow slow and grow deep. Growing fast doesn't always equate to velocity and reorders.

Chris Joseph is CEO of Cascade Spirits

CHAPTER **NINE**

Business Life Cycle

Every business goes through phases, which can be boiled down to four major steps: startup, adolescence, maturity, and exit. Each phase will look and feel different for each company, but in essence the life cycle is the same.

One of the first choices that a business makes is to choose an entity type. In my experience, this is the biggest decision that receives the smallest amount of forethought from business owners. This choice can be rushed or overlooked for various reasons. In the early days, the owner is excited to get going, looks for the fastest path to start producing, and will say yes to anything just begin living his or her dream.Imagine a potential investor requests changes to an operating agreement prior to signing on, and the founder does little to question or push back on the requested changes because she is so close to having all the capital needed to finally get the distillery up and running. Another common scenario is that a fifty-fifty ownership split is agreed upon between two partners, when in fact, one party is bringing more to the table than the other. These scenarios can cause frustration in the future, but with proper planning many headaches can be avoided.

As a business owner is in the planning phase it is important to understand the differences between entity types. If a business is already established when undesirable aspects of its legal structure come to light, fear not! The business is not stuck with that entity type forever; it *can* be changed. However, the process to switch entity types can get complicated and is not always easy to do, and it can trigger tax liabilities. Best case scenario: think through the organization type before establishing the company. This will position it for success and may avoid future challenges.

There are many long-term consequences that are difficult to foresee until the moment when they arise, but the more a founder knows about the different entity types, the better prepared he or she will be when setting up the organization. This section is a brief overview of the different structures. As a caveat, the reader must remember that I am not an attorney, nor do I hold myself out as such. I strongly recommend working with a business attorney who can help navigate these choices from a legal perspective. I also recommend consulting a CPA to gain an understanding of any tax implications for each entity choice.

Traditional choices of entity include single member LLC, sole proprietorship partnership, S corporation, and C corporation. We will also discuss B corporations, which at the time of writing have no unique legal or tax characteristics. Note that this is not an exhaustive list of the available entity types.

SINGLE MEMBER LLC

A **single member LLC** is a business that is owned by one party. The party that owns the business may be an individual or another partnership or corporation. Single member LLCs are considered a *disregarded entity* because they file no tax return of their own. Instead, the financial results are reported on the tax return of the parent organization. For example, if Sally Jones is the sole owner of Anderson Distillery, she can report Anderson Distillery on Schedule C of her individual tax return (Form 1040). Anderson Distillery would not file a tax return of its own, even though it has its own TIN (tax identification number).

The benefit of a single member LLC structure is its simplicity. It's easy to establish and report. The drawback is there is no opportunity to include others as owners. One party bears 100% of the risk (yet also stands to gain 100% of the reward). To raise capital from other individuals, or go into business with more than one person, the single member LLC structure is not the right choice.

The income or loss of a single member LLC is taxed at the individual level of the owner; there is no entity-level income tax.

SOLE PROPRIETORSHIP

A **sole proprietorship** is the simplest way to organize a business. It is run by only one person under his own name or a trade name. There is no formal entity to designate the assets of the business from the assets of the owner. All income and expenses are reported on the individual's personal income tax return, and the individual will pay both income tax and self-employment tax on any earnings from the activity. While simple to establish, this plan should be used only for businesses in the very early stages of their life cycle, or businesses that have very little liability exposure.

Let's go back to the example of Sally Jones from the section above. She could have chosen to start a distillery without formally establishing an LLC, instead of creating the LLC for Anderson Distillery. She could register with the TTB and register with the Secretary of State without establishing an LLC. However, her entire personal assets would be at risk, whereas with the LLC a legal shield provides some separation from personal assets versus business assets.

While possible to open a business as a sole proprietorship, I strongly advise against this format. It is the riskiest of all entity types available because there is no delineation between business and personal activity. Establishing an LLC shield is important because it segregates the assets of the business from the personal assets. If the business fails and creditors are looking to collect on amounts owed, they can reach only to the business assets, while personal assets remain protected. Another particularly important consideration, especially in the context of a spirits business, is protection if a consumer sues the organization. Imagine a patron imbibing at a tasting room. She leaves the premises and gets into a car accident. If she sued the company for overserving, only the business assets would be within reach; personal assets would not be exposed.

***AUTHOR'S NOTE:** It's important to note that forming an LLC or corporate shield will not always protect personal assets. The more sophisticated the creditor, the more likely that an individual owner/operator will be required to sign a personal guarantee for company debt. A classic example is a bank loan for equipment purchases. It's quite likely that the bank would require anyone who owns 20% or more of the business, or who materially participates in the company, to guarantee the loan personally. This means he or she is on the hook to repay the debt if for some reason the business cannot fulfill that obligation.*

PARTNERSHIP

A **partnership** exists when two or more persons or entities come together to own a business. In essence, a partnership has no corpus of its own. Instead, it is the sum of efforts and resources of the owners. An important note: the equity section of a partnership's balance sheet displays only partner capital accounts and no retained earnings. This presentation demonstrates that there is no equity of the company itself; all earnings or losses are allocated ratably among the partners.

Ownership in a partnership is expressed in units. From a legal perspective, partnerships are quite flexible. Partners could write almost anything they want into the partnership agreement and it would be valid if all partners agree to it. Because of the flexibility of the organizational structure, it is often used in business.

Partnerships also are a common structure when one primary partner has the vision or core skills, but lacks the money. Because of the flexibility of partnerships, the primary partner can collect money from investors, while limiting decision-making power of the investors. These limitations are expressed in Class A and Class B units. It is common for a partnership to establish classes of investment that have different rights over day-to-day operations. By employing different classes of units, the primary partner mitigates the risk that her decisions will be overridden by investors.

A partnership can include general partners and limited partners. General partners are liable for company debt, whereas limited partners are not. A limited partner is at risk only of losing the amount of money that he has invested.

There is also a characteristic of material participation that distinguishes partners. Material participation means that an individual is actively involved in the operations of the company. The alternative to material participation is passive investment. A passive investor does not participate in day-to-day management; generally speaking, a passive investor has contributed capital and is waiting for a return in the form of distributions or gain upon their exit from the company. Both general partners and limited partners can materially participate.

The distinction of material participation versus passive investment is important because the ability to deduct certain categories of expenses for tax purposes is limited if a partner is passive. Additionally, partners who materially participate are subject to self-employment tax on income allocated to them from the business, whereas passive investors are not subject to self-employment tax.

From a tax perspective, partnerships are flow-through entities. A flow-through entity has no entity-level income tax. While it does file a tax return, all elements of income or loss are reported to the individual owners on a Form K-1. The information on the Form K-1 is reported on each owner's personal tax return and is subject to tax at the individual level.

The downside to partnerships is that the tax law surrounding them is complex and can become even more complex depending on the specific language of the operating agreement. Another negative aspect is that a member participating in the company operations is subject to self-employment tax on the amount of income allocated to her. Note that any person who has ownership — even a small percentage — should receive a K-1 only; it is technically incorrect for someone to receive both a K-1 and a W-2 from the same company.

Frequently, distillers will offer equity to key employees. Upon becoming an equity holder, a key employee should cease to receive a W-2 and should instead receive a K-1. Self-employment tax is the equivalent of the social security and Medicare tax to which every W-2 employee is subject.

S CORPORATION

A corporation that elects S status is deemed an S corporation. S corporations are, like partnerships, a flow-through entity. Ownership in an S corporation is expressed in shares. Unlike partnerships, they are much more stringent in rules related to how they can be organized. Per IRS regulations, S corporations must:

- Be a domestic corporation
- Have only allowable shareholders
  - May be individuals, certain trusts, and estates and
  - May not be partnerships, corporations or non-resident alien shareholders
- Have no more than 100 shareholders
- Have only one class of stock
- Not be an ineligible corporation (i.e. certain financial institutions, insurance companies, and domestic international sales corporations)

The restriction of having one class of stock can be problematic for entities that are seeking to raise capital without giving away decision-making rights, as discussed above. In a partnership, a business can have multiple classes of units. Class A units may be reserved for founders and may have the right to financial benefits as well as decision-making rights, whereas Class B units may have the right to financial benefits only and no decision-making rights. This is often a valuable provision for founders because it allows them to raise money but not give up the decision-making control.

***AUTHOR'S NOTE:** Scenario comparison: In Table 9.1 we have presented the tax scenario for a partnership or sole proprietorship vs an S corporation. For this purpose, we assume that the Federal income tax rate is 30% and self-employment tax is 15.3%. In our scenario, an owner receives a salary of $60,000. The company also has net income — after considering the salary to the owner - o f which, $40,000 is allocated to the owner.*

In an S corp, any individual who works for a company must receive a W-2, even if he holds equity. This is a big difference between partnerships and S corps. This requirement may be burdensome for small companies. Imagine a distillery owned by a husband and wife with no other employees. In order to receive

Table 9.1

PARTNERSHIP OR SOLE PROPRIETORSHIP			
Guaranteed Payments	$60,000	Subject to income tax and self-employment tax	$27,180 *($60,000 * (30%+15.3%))*
Net Income Allocation	$40,000	Subject to income tax and self-employment tax	$18,120 *($40,000 * (30%+15.3%))*
Total tax			$45,300 total tax
Net after tax			$54,700
S CORPORATION			
Wages	$60,000	Subject to income tax and employee portion of employment tax	$22,590 *($60,000 * (30%+7.65%))*
Net Income Allocation	$40,000	Subject to income tax	$12,000 *($40,000 * 30%)*
Total tax			$34,590 total tax
Net after tax			$65,410

a salary, they both must be on payroll. This means that the company will have to process payroll and file payroll tax returns (an additional expense), whereas if they were organized as a partnership the husband and wife would simply take guaranteed payments from the company which do not require payroll tax returns to be filed. Note that the additional expense of processing payroll is a disadvantage only until the company has other employees besides the owners. Once other employees are hired it becomes a moot point because payroll will need to be processed in order to report the employee wages correctly.

Under current tax law, one major advantage of S corporations is that owners may take distributions that are exempt from self-employment tax. To illustrate: The owner/operator of a distillery receives a salary of $60,000 that is reported on a W-2, and at the end of the year also takes a distribution of $40,000. Social security and Medicare tax will be withheld from the regular payroll checks (the $60,000); however, the distribution of $40,000 is not subject to payroll tax. Currently this plan represents a savings of 7.65% (1.45% for Medicare tax, and 6.2% of social security tax (subject to wage limitations)). This benefit can be a compelling factor when considering the best structure for an entity.

The IRS requires that distributions be reasonable in amount relative to W-2 wages. For example, an owner should not take $20,000 in wages and $80,000 in distributions for a total compensation of $100,000. In that scenario, the IRS would be missing out on the Social Security and Medicare tax revenue from any wages paid (except for the $20,000 reported on the W-2).

Finding the correct balance for S corp owners of what should be reported on payroll versus what can be taken as a distribution is a balancing act and should be discussed with the owner's personal CPA.

***AUTHOR'S NOTE:** In my opinion, a small business should elect S corporation status if there is enough cash flow from operations that the owner-operators can pay themselves a reasonable salary and have cash left over to issue distributions to the shareholders.*

C CORPORATION

A **C corporation** is not a flow-through entity. Corporations are deemed to be an independent entity and pay their own taxes. Ownership in C corporations is expressed in shares. One of the biggest drawbacks of a C corporation is that, under current tax law, income from C corporations is subject to double taxation. If an entity reports taxable income, then the entity itself pays tax. If the corporation also issues dividends to its stockholders, those dividends are subject to tax at the individual level. Thus, two layers of tax.

In 2017 US Congress overhauled the IRS code. Prior to changes in the tax code, the cumulative tax rate to income from corporations was quite high. However, after the tax changes in 2017, the corporate rate was lowered significantly, resulting in a cumulative tax rate that is comparable to income taxed from a flow-through entity. For that reason, many investors who previously chose to avoid C corporations due to double taxation are now giving the structure a second look.

There are other tax provisions that might make a C corporation attractive to investors, one of which is small business stock (Section 1202 of the IRS code). Under this rule, qualified small business stock can be liquidated with no capital gain tax on any gain.

***AUTHOR'S NOTE:** Tax legislation can change at any time and rates or rules expressed in this text may not be accurate in the future. Always check with your tax advisor to get updated guidance.*

B CORPORATION

The B in B corporation stands for benefit. While a B corporation has no meaning in a tax or legal aspect, it may be desirable for business owners who want to recognize their standards towards being a steward for their employees, the community and their environment. Many businesses view B corp certification as an important factor for attracting and retaining employees and customers.

AUTHOR'S NOTE: MORE ABOUT LLCs

Businesses have a legal structure and a tax determination. There is not a one-to-one relationship. A corporation is a legal structure. By default, it is taxed as a C corporation and files a Form 1120. However, the company may elect to be taxed as an S corporation. The election is a request that is made to the Internal Revenue Service. If the IRS accepts the request, then the company is deemed an S corporation for tax purposes and files a Form 1120S.

A similar distinction exists for LLCs. For legal purposes, a company may choose to be a limited liability company (LLC). By default, an LLC is taxed as a partnership and files a Form 1065; however, the LLC may elect to be taxed as a C corp, in which it would file a Form 1120, or an S corp, in which it would file a Form 1120S.

BUSINESS LIFE CYCLE

All organizations experience different phases of their corporate life. The phases of a life cycle include start-up, adolescence, maturity, and decline. How much time a particular business spends in each stage depends on a myriad of factors, but as a general rule, all organizations follow the same pattern. Some organizations may last for one year, and others may last for hundreds of years. In this section, we will describe characteristics of each phase and how its impact on the finances of an organization.

Figure 9.1, from CorporateFinanceInstitute.com, illustrates the corporate life cycle.

In start-up phase, an owner is proving the concept of the business. This phase involves writing a business plan, raising capital, purchasing equipment, making initial hires, and making early sales. From a financial perspective, the company is spending more than it is bringing in. Most activity in the start-up phase is on the balance sheet. Some examples include:

- trading equity for cash
- trading cash for equipment
- building inventory
- incurring debt

Generally, a distillery will incur a net loss on its income statement for, on average, the first seven years. This occurs because a lot of investment goes towards the team and the process before sales can start. Of course, the timeline is dependent on the spirits

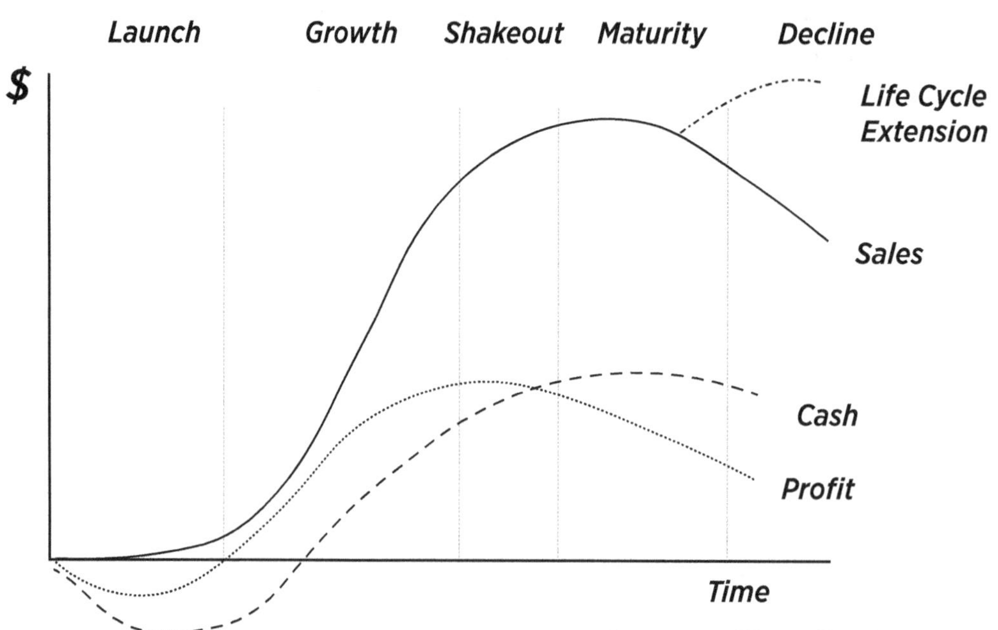

Figure 9.1

Image courtesy of CorporateFinanceInstitute.com

being produced: the more aging involved, the more time required before product can be sold; therefore achieving profitability takes longer than if a company is selling white spirits. Once the sales commence, they are usually slow to come on until the distillery reaches a certain point of popularity with the brand. This growth is demonstrated in consistent and predictable orders from customers, and a constant stream of patrons in a tasting room.

Many spirits producers mitigate the early-year losses by buying spirits in bulk from another producer and layering in their own blending before taking a product to market. This is one way to shorten the timeline to profitability. Some purists may balk at the idea of selling someone else's product as their own, but that is a philosophical debate we will leave for another day.

Once a company emerges out of start-up, it enters adolescence. In this phase, a company is growing — in terms of sales, in terms of the number of team members, and in terms of the physical production facility. Revenue often grows rapidly. It is common for a company to incur losses in the early part of adolescence, and it is within the adolescence phase when a company turns profitable. Adolescence is a time of expansion. As growth occurs, the company must continue to invest in raw materials and inventory, and often for barrel-aged products, this means an expansion of storage space to give enough room for additional product to age. Net income percentages can fluctuate up and down during these years, but generally trend upward.

In maturity, revenue growth slows and follows closer to an economy's macro-level growth. Net income percentages decline, and business operations stabilize. To create spikes in revenue or income, spirits producers may experiment with product innovation or industry trends. The equilibrium of a mature company can sustain for a short or long period of time.

Eventually there is a decline or exit of some sort. This could be a liquidation event in which the distillery sells to another, or the company could wind down operations. In this phase, operations, assets, revenue, and profit all decline.

WHEN TO HIRE

Through a company's life cycle, personnel needs will ebb and flow. Like all departments of the distillery, the accounting department will evolve over time. There are a few key hires that will be essential as the company matures: bookkeeper, Controller, CFO.

***AUTHOR'S NOTE:** As a general rule, I believe that if you can keep someone utilized for 70% of the time, then you should hire the position full time. If you don't have enough work to keep someone busy more than 70% of the time, you are likely better off outsourcing the work. While outsourcing may be more expensive on an hourly basis, it does give the freedom to get specific about the level of talent that is needed. If you need a bookkeeper for 30 hours a week, an accounting manager for 8 hours a week, and a Controller for 10 hours a month, you can get that through an outsourced solution. And you will not be paying payroll tax or benefits. Flexibility in skill set declines if an employee is hired full time.*

Bookkeepers are responsible for recording transactions into the company's accounting system. The types of transactions a bookkeeper normally handles include recording sales, purchases, payroll data, and other operating expenses. A bookkeeper may also be responsible for reconciling accounts at the end of the month. Generally, a bookkeeper's work will be reviewed by an accounting manager or some other senior position. He may also participate in the budget process by aggregating information from multiple departments into one budget.

A qualified bookkeeper should have a few years of experience working under the supervision of a more seasoned professional, ideally a CPA. Bookkeepers should be proficient in the software used for financial recordkeeping, have an understanding of the spirits industry, and keep strong attention to detail.

Bookkeepers are the front-line employees of the accounting department. They generally interface with employees from other departments. As is said, 'garbage in, garbage out,' and bookkeepers are the custodians of what goes into the system. For that reason, having a smart, capable bookkeeper is an incredibly important role for any small business.

A **Controller** oversees the development and implementation of the accounting system. He or she may supervise bookkeepers, staff accountants, and/or accounting managers depending on the size and scope of the organization.

The Controller is responsible for setting internal controls. Internal controls are processes and procedures that mitigate the risk of fraudulent acts.

Controllers serve as the quality control mechanism of an accounting department. This role is managerial, and a successful Controller should have at least 5 years accounting experience, be adept at operating accounting software, understand GAAP rules, and have a good understanding of the spirits industry and regulated environment.

A Chief Financial Officer (**CFO**) is responsible for leading long-term, sustainable financial success of the company. The CFO links owners' or Board of Directors' objectives to the business. The CFO analyzes data and provides recommendations that enable the leadership team to make decisions.

A CFO establishes the short- and long-term financial strategy in service to the organizational strategy and heavily influences the organization's risk appetite. The CFO manages performance, and drives decision-making. He or she is the financially-grounded business navigator who understands the specific business and the industry in which it operates. The CFO creates, reports, and preserves value.

Skills needed from a CFO include strategic development, risk mitigation and assessment, capital and resource allocation, strategy implementation, talent identification, assessment and development, and ability to establish compensation systems. A CFO aligns KPIs to outcomes, provides business support such as scenario planning (e.g., what will be the effect if we raise our prices?), and produces accurate, timely, and relevant financial reports. The CFO is also relied on to drive cost leadership, improve productivity, appraise potential investments, manage tax planning, manage cash flow, oversee internal controls, and communicate business performance to stakeholders. A CFO should be able to communicate complex ideas clearly, build relationships with other department leaders, and have solid project management skills.

The soft skills needed of a CFO are as important as the technical skills. A CFO should set the appropriate tone, articulate a clear vision of financial management, and be forward thinking. The CFO should act with integrity, credibility and influence. Successful CFOs offer constructive feedback to other leaders, root recommendations in objective data, and operate ethically.

In terms of influence, the CFO has an effect on external parties such as customers, business partners, community and environmental stakeholders, regulators and shareholders. This individual also has an effect on internal parties such as the Board of Directors, senior management, cross-departmental colleagues, peers, and employees who report to him or her.

Understanding the corporate life cycle is critical for a distillery's management. Seeing a particular company in the context of a larger lens can lead to better decision-making.

Real-Life Application

Governing Documents

Every company has a governing document that sets for the rules of engagement for the entity. In limited liability companies this is called the Operating Agreement; in corporations it is called the Articles of Incorporation. For our purposes in the following interview we will refer to Operating Agreement, but the concepts apply to all entity types.

Creating the governing document is one of the first tasks of a start-up, and I always encourage company founders to work with an attorney who is well versed in the beverage alcohol industry and with the intricacies of various business entity types. The guiding hand of your attorney is critical at this stage of a company's development. To get insight on operating agreements, I sat down with Marcus Reed. Marcus is attorney based in Portland, Oregon who specializes in the beverage alcohol industry.

Pearman: Thanks, Marcus, for sitting down to discuss common issues in partnership agreements. You have written many operating agreements for beverage alcohol companies and have great experience to share. In the history of my practice, I have seen a lot of founders get into trouble when drafting an operating agreement because they are so excited to just get going with making whatever they're making — beer, spirits, wine, cider — that they accept any terms in order to get the operation off the ground. Legal terms are accepted without considering the long-term consequences of them. What are your suggestions for structuring the operating agreement drafting process to ensure that important considerations are thoroughly vetted?

Reed: When writing an operating agreement, one of the major considerations is how decisions will be made within a company, and who has the ability to make different types of decisions. Company decisions are not always going to be made by the majority owner, and companies should certainly avoid a 50/50 situation in which every disagreement is going to need a tie-breaker.

Operating agreements should differentiate between the types of decisions that are to be made and who is going to be making those decisions. There's really no fixed way to do that — it's kind of a process each founder must go through. He or she needs to decide what is important and be able to have the decision-making authority on those very important topics. Oftentimes decision-making rights are going to be for active owners of the company who are involved in operations. They will want more of the operational control of the company; passive members might want more control over things like changes of ownership.

Common distinctions for business matters that may be called out in an operating agreement include the purchase of assets over a certain value, or entering into certain types of agreements, such as agreements to acquire real estate. These matters often require the permission of members. In other words, a managing member cannot make these types of decisions without asking first for a vote from the decision-making class of members. The larger the decision, the more likely the operating agreement will call for support from a majority, super majority, or unanimity. Many operating agreements also have a section that lists the types of decisions that can be made unilaterally by the operating manager.

Pearman: How do you feel about allowing potential investors to make proposed changes to operating agreements? Do you recommend that not be an option?

Reed: It is usually going to depend on the level of investment that the investors are making. If it is a significant financial investment, and if the start-up needs this investor, they will probably be more willing to negotiate with them on operating agreement terms. If it is not a significant financial commitment, or maybe you have a number of investors coming in as minority investors and you want to apply the same rules to everybody, then individual investors will have less negotiating leverage.

Investors should be cognizant of the effect that their level of oversight is going to have on the day-to-day management. The concerns of investors are usually the big ticket items that have the potential to change the nature of the business in some way. For example, taking on a new product line entirely, or opening a new location -- the big things that pose a risk to the business or somehow dilute their ownership. Otherwise, in my opinion, investors shouldn't care. And if they do care about the day-to-day and they want to micromanage, then they may not be a good fit for the company.

Pearman Let's talk about provisions in an operating agreement for distributions. I frequently see operating agreements that include priority returns. Investors want to be paid back for their capital investment first before there's common share of distributions with the operating owner. I think a lot of founders find themselves in a situation that catches them off guard. They get to a year in which the company is profitable and they realize that they as owner-operators are not participating in distributions in the same way as some of the other financial investors. That realization can cause a lot of bad feelings and undue stress. What do you think founders should watch out for in terms of language for those waterfall distributions, and how that plays out in real life?

Reed: Those provisions are challenging because that is often going to be the draw for an investor. They want to have priority rights to distributions so that they get their investment back. I think one way to deal with that is make sure that those priority rights are going to sunset at some point, where maybe after a portion of their investment has been repaid, and they feel they have reclaimed some or all of what they put into the investment, the priority rights go away and they become the same class as the founders or whoever has their less priority rights. But sometimes the guarantee of priority rights is what it takes to get investors on board.

Pearman: Thanks for sharing your thoughts on those elements of the operating agreement. Clear guidelines for who has the power to make decisions, and for how distributions are shared can have significant downstream effects on a business. I appreciate you sharing your expertise.

Real-Life Application

Organizational Structure and Distributor Agreement Considerations

I sat down with Shauna Barnes, a beverage alcohol attorney, to get her perspective on legal considerations for distilleries. Shauna is a partner at Kaleo Legal. Prior to her current firm she was the General Counsel of Dogfish Head Brewery in Delaware. She represents breweries, wineries and distilleries, and estimates that 25%-30% of her work is with distilleries. Here are her thoughts on the state of the industry, recommendations for organizational structure, and distributor agreements.

I am seeing more breweries expand into spirits. Of those crossing sectors most want to do an RTD [ready to drink cocktail], or to release a whiskey. I'd say that 75% want to release an RTD; the other 25% want to do whiskey. However, the trend doesn't go the other way. I am not seeing distillers expand into beer.

As relates to organizational structure, most companies are either a C corporation or LLC [limited liability company]. If a company has aspirations to be acquired, they usually choose to form as a C corporation because it is an attractive corporate structure in the eyes of investors. On the other hand, founders who establish a distillery because it's their dream tend to be an LLC.

When setting up corporate structure, many aspects need consideration. Each type of structure has long term implications. That isn't to say that a structure is written in stone once established, but to change it may not be as easy as you think.

One issue that deserves special consideration is investor relations — what I like to call "investor care and feeding". An LLC is a more flexible entity than a corporation, and so it can be easier to raise capital if your company is an LLC, but that also requires the company to issue a K-1 to all investors and possibly to issue tax distributions. A C corporation, on the other hand, does not have the same issues. Also consider the number of investors involved. If you are planning to raise money from 40 individuals, that could require a lot more care and feeding than if you raised money from 2 or 3 individuals.

If a distillery has several investors it can sometimes be better to be a corporation because the entity does not have to disclose as much personal information to the TTB [Alcohol Tax and Trade Bureau].

If organized as a partnership, the distillery must disclose a significant amount of information about all members, regardless of their percentage interest. The personnel questionnaire that is required by the TTB is a bit of an invasive document. Among other information, the questionnaire asks for a member's name, Social Security number, and detailed financial information. This includes disclosing history from your personal financial records. An investor is basically giving the regulatory authorities his or her entire banking history. We've had clients with potential investors who were interested because they saw it as a fun opportunity, but after educating them on the required disclosures they no longer wanted to invest. In fact, the requested information sometimes borders on the ridiculous. I once had a client who had to disclose the CEO's wife's weight to get an importer license. Each state has different requirements, and that was in the state of California. You can see how this can become quite awkward.

As a practitioner, I generally don't like partnerships. I think that even with a well-written partnership agreement, partnerships are more likely to get into bigger dissolution fights than those entities organized as a corporation. I think it's all based on the legal documentation, and as a partnership there is less protection under the law. I always push clients to be an LLC or a C corporation if they anticipate having more than one investor.

My number one piece of advice for a distillery in planning is to think about what the breakup looks like. It may sound pessimistic, but I speak from experience. When you are doing your entity formation and writing the operating agreement, consider how you are going to decide if there are only two partners who don't agree. We've found that if partners talk about these kinds of issues before even coming to us, they save money on attorney fees and it's a cleaner papering process. I strongly encourage business partners to talk about the difficult questions up front. We don't want to bill people for time spent on an entity that ultimately doesn't launch.

Let's change gears and talk about another critical legal consideration. That is, distributor agreements. Will this affect every distillery? Probably not, because it depends on the business model.

If a distillery's model is to have a tasting room as the primary revenue stream, with off-premise sales to support the brand, wait until the brand is big enough that people are clamoring for the product before engaging with a distributor.

If your model is traditional — that is, heavily dependent on wholesale sales — you should be selling to a traditional wine/spirits distributor. It's important to look for a distributor who has a proven ability to service liquor stores.

Another model to consider is a brewer who decides to enter liquor category. A brewer who wants to add a canned cocktail will have different considerations when choosing a distributor than a brewer who wants to add a line of whiskey. If adding an RTD, you may want to be with a beer distributor because RTDs are consumed at beer drinking locations. However, if you are introducing a new line of whiskey you may want to be with a spirits distributor who is better positioned to service those retail accounts.

What's your distillery's model and purpose? Tasting room, traditional, RTD? We spend a lot of time with clients discussing what will be sold, defining the market, where it will be purchased, and where it will be consumed. All aspects are important keys to choosing the right distributor. Remember that a traditional spirits distributor is very different than a beer distributor.

And just because franchise law doesn't apply to distilleries does not mean the distributor isn't going to want some protection. I encourage all distillers to establish a [distribution] contract in every state where they sell product. Watch out for wholesalers who will attempt to lock a supplier into a franchise-type contract, despite the fact that franchise law doesn't apply.

A common development is for suppliers to ask distributors is to invest in their brand by way of an agreed upon termination fee. If the distributor terminates the agreement before the term is over, you are paid something. It becomes a consideration of how long a term are they getting for distribution, what will they invest in the brand, does the supplier think it's fair? You need basic terms and conditions, and you have to begin as you mean to go on. I think any brand can receive at least a small amount of consideration to compensate for the brand being locked up with one distributor for a few years.

Like a business's operating agreement, most of these distributor agreements are important because they are setting the terms of the breakup. It is effectively a buyout agreement and most of the language relates to what will happen if things don't work out.

While the legal aspects of a business may not always be the most exciting parts, they are often the most important. I strongly encourage distillery owners to take careful consideration of their choices related to entity formation and distributor agreements. Think things through, consider all angles, and invest in good counsel!

CHAPTER **TEN**

Finance Options

It is a rare company that doesn't worry about financing at some point in their life cycle. Most companies reach a point at which ambition outstrips resources and money has to be raised or borrowed to advance to the next level. This chapter introduces various finance options and how to determine the most favorable option. Finance encompasses the topics of funding sources, capital structuring, and investment decisions. There are a few key concepts to understand about finance.

1. ***Time Value of Money***
   Time value of money is the concept that money decreases in value over time due to its earning capacity, which relates to inflation. A dollar today is worth more than a dollar tomorrow. An investor would prefer to have cash now instead of later because a today's dollar can be invested and make money. The formula for computing time value of money considers the current outflow, the future value, the interest rate, and time.

2. ***Risk-Return Tradeoff***
   Risk-return tradeoff is the concept that potential return of an investment is inversely related to its risk. Invested money can render higher profits if the investor will accept a higher possibility of losses. The risk of an investment opportunity should be considered as an isolated event and in aggregate of an entire investment portfolio.

3. ***Cost of Capital***
   Cost of capital is the required return on investment to make a project worthwhile.

If funding is comprised of both debt and equity, cost of capital is a blended rate of both components, also known as weighted average cost of capital. This is often referred to by its acronym, WACC. How much return is needed on a project so that the return exceeds the investment? For example, if a $100,000 project is financed with 50% debt with a 5% APR and 50% equity with an 8% hurdle rate, then the annual return would need to be more than $6,500 annually:
(5+8)/2 = 6.5% x $100,000 = $6,500.

4. ***Interest Rate***
   Interest rate is the percentage rate charged for the use of assets. It is expressed as a percentage, which is multiplied by the principal of the asset. Interest rate is usually expressed as an annual percentage rate (APR). For example, 18% APR is the same as 1.5% monthly interest. (1.5 x 12 = 18). Interest can be defined in more detail as simple interest or compound interest.

Simple interest is calculated by multiplying the interest rate by the principal by the number of days between payments.

AUTHOR'S NOTE: If $100,000 is borrowed at simple interest of 18% for six months, then the interest for the borrowed period is $9,000. $100,000 * 18% * 183/365 = $9,000

Compound interest is calculated by multiplying the interest rate by the sum of the principal *plus* the accumulated interest of previous periods. Compounding periods can be any set amount of time, and generally will be annually, quarterly, monthly, or daily.

AUTHOR'S NOTE: If $100,000 is borrowed at a rate of 18% and if interest compounds annually, then the total interest paid on the $100,000 will be $18,000 per year. (This assumes the interest expense is paid. If interest isn't paid, then the interest becomes part of the principal.) If interest compounds at some other frequency, such as quarterly, the interest paid on the $100,000 will be:

$100,000 * 18% * 3 months = $4,500

$104,500 * 18% * 3 months = $4,702.50

$109,202.50 * 18% * 3 months = $4,914.11

$114,116.61 * 18% * 3 months = $5,135.25

Total interest for the year = $19,251.86 (or 19.25% of the principal).

5. ***Capital Budgeting***
   Capital budgeting is the process used to evaluate a major investment. Generally, it involves analyzing a project's long term cash flows and calculation of ROI (return on investment) versus the hurdle rate. Hurdle rate is the required return that a project must meet before being approved by company leadership. There are multiple methods of measuring a capital project's return. Some of the more common methods are discounted cash flow analysis, which accounts for initial costs, expected inflows, and ongoing costs; payback analysis, which measures how long it will take to recoup the initial investment; and throughput analysis, which considers how the investment will affect the organization as a whole.

ANALYZING INVESTMENT OPTIONS

Once financing options have been identified, a company should analyze each to get a full understanding of the cost involved and the effects of the finance option on the company's financial health. In this section we cover discounted cash flow analysis — a very common method of analyzing the return on a project.

Net present value (NPV) determines the future cash flows from an investment. Net present value calculation is also referred to as discounted cash flow analysis (DCF). As an equation it is expressed as:

DCF = (CF1/(1+r)1) + (CF2/(1+r)2) + … + (CFn/(1+r)n)

Real-Life Application

Nontraditional Finance Options for Distilleries

The financing options for small businesses have come a long way in most recent decade. It's common that companies in a growth phase find themselves past the emerging stage of their corporate life cycle, but they aren't yet bankable by a traditional bank. And this predicament isn't just limited to early-stage producers. Beverage alcohol financier Quinton Jay gives an overview of financing options beyond the usual institutional debt.

The big takeaway is that the world is now offers the option of non-traditional banks. This is a different ecosystem than FDIC-backed banks. Non-traditional banks, also known as alternative lenders, are not regulated by the Federal government. Most small businesses get started with funds from friends and family. That gets them through start-up, and then there's another wave of cash needed for expansion. The next round of financing usually goes beyond friends and family, and the money has a higher cost of capital. The cost of capital is primarily based on risk, and small businesses have a higher risk profile. Alternative lenders can offer financing options when a company has exhausted start-up funds, but isn't yet bankable in the eyes of a traditional institution.

The lenders' regulations are different than banks because they are not federally regulated. Most traditional banks are purely based on a cash flow lending model and if you are growing you may not have positive cash flow. Maybe you are spending it on inventory, sales, or whatever, but you are burning cash. That's where these non-traditional banks and alternative lenders come in.

Alternative lenders come in all sort of shapes and sizes. Some specialize in a particular sales channel like direct-to-consumer business models; some specialize in a particular industry. They may know a vertical really well and be able to train the financing to something useful for that particular borrower.

The path to an alternative lender is not necessarily a straight line. The best place to start is with a traditional lender. You've got to first get turned down by traditional banks; almost everyone starts by approaching the banks first. If a traditional bank isn't interested in financing your company, they may have contacts at non-traditional banks. Through research and recommendations, you will find someone for your specialty. For example, one of my clients currently uses Assembled Brands, who specializes in direct-to-consumer channels. There are other lenders like this, too. When you are in that community of the non-traditional lenders, one will be able to recommend others.

Going with a non-traditional lender will be more expensive money than a traditional lender. You're looking at sometimes up to 1% interest per month. There can also be a commitment fee and possibly a monthly monitoring fee. You have some of those fees with traditional banks, but they are usually negotiable. Traditional banks are lending money at around 4-6%; non-traditional banks are double on average.

Some business owners are concerned about engaging with an alternative lender. They worry that it will be a red flag if another investor sees they have borrowed from a non-traditional bank. That's not necessarily the case. One caveat is merchant credit advances lenders (MCAs). In my experience, some lenders may take pause if they see that a company had borrowed money from an MCA. Many MCAs are providing multiple services to a small business. For example, Shopify Capital is a related company to Shopify, a service that many companies use for their online stores. Shopify Capital is a non-traditional lender. It lends based on your inventory and also on your daily sales. There are many big corporations who have operations in MCAs (American Express, PayPal, Quickbooks). Quickbooks Capital is seemingly a conflict because they have full access to your books and then decide if they are going to lend to you.

The primary drawback to MCA loans is the way those loans are structured. A borrower is often locked into terms that are a longer repayment period (and thus more interest expense) than is really needed. Let's say you need money for three months during a cash crunch — it's October through December and you need to load up on inventory for the holiday season, but sales won't hit until the end of the year. So, you are in need for a short period of time — three months. Unfortunately, the terms are often longer than three months; the terms are six months, or even twelve months. Even if you don't need the money that long, you have to pay for the longer term. To expand on the example above, a company needs money in Q4 but is flush with cash in January. With MCAs you keep paying interest for the whole term even if you could pay it off earlier.

Alternative financing options have proliferated over the last several years, and they can be a useful lifeline for companies if used responsibly. My advice is to thoroughly vet an option like this before jumping in. Go into any agreements with alternative lenders with eyes wide open.

where CF represents cash flow for a particular period; r is the interest rate for a particular period; and n is the number of future periods that include cash flows from the project.

Discounted cash flow analysis is helpful for business leaders who are deciding among multiple options of potential investments. It expresses in quantitative terms the investment options that will create the most value for shareholders. It provides a level playing field on which to compare various options, regardless of the timing of cash flows. Businesses should accept options with a positive NPV and decline options with a negative NPV. (A positive NPV means that a project will provide return that exceeds the initial investment; a negative NPV means a project will lose money.) NPV is the cash flows of a particular project, which is then discounted to arrive at a future value. Net present value is one of the most common decision-making tools used for capital budgeting.

Example: evaluating multiple options for equipment financing.

Assume the following scenario: a distillery is considering spending $150,000 on equipment that will result in increased production capacity and an additional $5,000 net profit per month. There are three options that the company is considering for financing the equipment purchase. In each option, we'll employ a calculation of net present value.

The first option is to fund the equipment through equity. That is, the company will raise $150,000 from investors.

The second option is to fund the equipment through debt. They have an offer from a lender who is allowing them to pay 10% down ($15,000) and finance the remainder. The terms of the loan are 5 years with an annual percentage rate (APR) of 5.5%. The third option is also debt, but with different terms. The lender is offering them $0 downpayment with 100% of the cost financed. The terms of the loan are 5 years with an APR of 5.5%.

For the first option we subtract the initial investment of $150,000 which is already in present value. In other words, there is no time between this moment and when the funds will be disbursed. Then we factor the hurdle rate of equity as the cost of capital. The hurdle rate is used as the cost of capital is because there is no interest expense to be considered — we are paying for the equipment up front. But we *could have* invested that same $150,000 in another project, so the required rate of any investment is considered our cost of capital. *(Table 10.1)*

For the second option we subtract the initial investment of $15,000 which is already in present value. Then we subtract the net present value of future loan payments, and factor the interest rate of the loan as cost of capital. *(Table 10.2)*

For the third option we will subtract the net present value of future loan payments. There is no current payment, so the only thing to subtract is the NPV of future payments. The interest rate of the loan will be factored as the cost of capital. *(Table 10.3)*

Running a net present value calculation for each finance option helps the business the true cost or return of a project once all interest expense and the value of future cash flows is accounted for.

FINANCING THROUGH TRADITIONAL LENDERS

Presenting finances to a bank when seeking funding is part art and part science. Before approaching potential lenders consider how much money is needed, then tailor a presentation for potential bankers that presents the company as an attractive customer to a bank. Consider not only current projects that need funding, but also how much money will be needed for near-term growth.

Banks consider a variety of quantitative and qualitative factors when considering deals. Quantitative factors include the amount and terms of the loan requested, and the borrower's financial position — both the business and the primary operators involved in the business. Qualitative factors include the environment of the industry, the character of the borrower, and the quality of the collateral.

If financing the purchase or equipment or real estate, the loan may be collateralized with those specific assets. However, if borrowing working capital — i.e., cash — there is no associated collateral. A loan with no collateral is therefore riskier than a loan that is collateralized.

Be prepared that a lender may require a personal guarantee on company debt. This often is required

Table 10.1 Simple Loan Calculator - Option A

	Enter values	
Loan amount	$ -	
Annual interest rate	0.00%	
Loan period in years	0.00	5
Start date of loan	6/25/2021	
Monthly payment		
Number of payments		
Total interest		
Total cost of loan		

No.	Payment Date	Beginning Balance	Payment	Principal	Interest	Ending Balance		Pmts only	Positive cash flows	Net cash flows
									NPV	$ 98,849
							6/25/2021	$ (150,000)		$ (150,000)
							7/25/2021	$ -	$ 5,000	$ 5,000
							8/24/2021	$ -	$ 5,000	$ 5,000
							9/23/2021	$ -	$ 5,000	$ 5,000
							10/23/2021	$ -	$ 5,000	$ 5,000
							11/22/2021	$ -	$ 5,000	$ 5,000
							12/22/2021	$ -	$ 5,000	$ 5,000
							1/21/2022	$ -	$ 5,000	$ 5,000

Table 10.2 Simple Loan Calculator - Option B

	Enter values
Loan amount	$135,000.00
Annual interest rate	5.50%
Loan period in years	5.00
Start date of loan	6/25/2021
Monthly payment	$2,578.66
Number of payments	60
Total interest	$19,719.41
Total cost of loan	$154,719.41
NPV	$112,163

No.	Payment Date	Beginning Balance	Payment	Principal	Interest
1	7/25/2021	$ 135,000.00	$ 2,578.66	$ 1,959.91	$ 618.75
2	8/25/2021	$ 133,040.09	$ 2,578.66	$ 1,968.89	$ 609.77
3	9/25/2021	$ 131,071.20	$ 2,578.66	$ 1,977.91	$ 600.74
4	10/25/2021	$ 129,093.29	$ 2,578.66	$ 1,986.98	$ 591.68
5	11/25/2021	$ 127,106.31	$ 2,578.66	$ 1,996.09	$ 582.57
6	12/25/2021	$ 125,110.22	$ 2,578.66	$ 2,005.24	$ 573.42
7	1/25/2022	$ 123,104.99	$ 2,578.66	$ 2,014.43	$ 564.23
8	2/25/2022	$ 121,090.56	$ 2,578.66	$ 2,023.66	$ 555.00
9	3/25/2022	$ 119,066.90	$ 2,578.66	$ 2,032.93	$ 545.72
10	4/25/2022	$ 117,033.97	$ 2,578.66	$ 2,042.25	$ 536.41
11	5/25/2022	$ 114,991.72	$ 2,578.66	$ 2,051.61	$ 527.05
12	6/25/2022	$ 112,940.11	$ 2,578.66	$ 2,061.01	$ 517.64
13	7/25/2022	$ 110,879.09	$ 2,578.66	$ 2,070.46	$ 508.20
14	8/25/2022	$ 108,808.63	$ 2,578.66	$ 2,079.95	$ 498.71
15	9/25/2022	$ 106,728.68	$ 2,578.66	$ 2,089.48	$ 489.17
16	10/25/2022	$ 104,639.20	$ 2,578.66	$ 2,099.06	$ 479.60
17	11/25/2022	$ 102,540.14	$ 2,578.66	$ 2,108.68	$ 469.98
18	12/25/2022	$ 100,431.46	$ 2,578.66	$ 2,118.35	$ 460.31
19	1/25/2023	$ 98,313.11	$ 2,578.66	$ 2,128.06	$ 450.60
20	2/25/2023	$ 96,185.06	$ 2,578.66	$ 2,137.81	$ 440.85
21	3/25/2023	$ 94,047.25	$ 2,578.66	$ 2,147.61	$ 431.05
22	4/25/2023	$ 91,899.64	$ 2,578.66	$ 2,157.45	$ 421.21
23	5/25/2023	$ 89,742.19	$ 2,578.66	$ 2,167.34	$ 411.32
24	6/25/2023	$ 87,574.85	$ 2,578.66	$ 2,177.27	$ 401.38
25	7/25/2023	$ 85,397.58	$ 2,578.66	$ 2,187.25	$ 391.41
26	8/25/2023	$ 83,210.33	$ 2,578.66	$ 2,197.28	$ 381.38
27	9/25/2023	$ 81,013.05	$ 2,578.66	$ 2,207.35	$ 371.31

		Pmts only	Positive cash flows	Net cash flows
EndingBalance	6/25/2021	$ (15,000)		$ (15,000)
$ 133,040.09	7/25/2021	$ (2,579)	$ 5,000	$ 2,421
$ 131,071.20	8/25/2021	$ (2,579)	$ 5,000	$ 2,421
$ 129,093.29	9/25/2021	$ (2,579)	$ 5,000	$ 2,421
$ 127,106.31	10/25/2021	$ (2,579)	$ 5,000	$ 2,421
$ 125,110.22	11/25/2021	$ (2,579)	$ 5,000	$ 2,421
$ 123,104.99	12/25/2021	$ (2,579)	$ 5,000	$ 2,421
$ 121,090.56	1/25/2022	$ (2,579)	$ 5,000	$ 2,421
$ 119,066.90	2/25/2022	$ (2,579)	$ 5,000	$ 2,421
$ 117,033.97	3/25/2022	$ (2,579)	$ 5,000	$ 2,421
$ 114,991.72	4/25/2022	$ (2,579)	$ 5,000	$ 2,421
$ 112,940.11	5/25/2022	$ (2,579)	$ 5,000	$ 2,421
$ 110,879.09	6/25/2022	$ (2,579)	$ 5,000	$ 2,421
$ 108,808.63	7/25/2022	$ (2,579)	$ 5,000	$ 2,421
$ 106,728.68	8/25/2022	$ (2,579)	$ 5,000	$ 2,421
$ 104,639.20	9/25/2022	$ (2,579)	$ 5,000	$ 2,421
$ 102,540.14	10/25/2022	$ (2,579)	$ 5,000	$ 2,421
$ 100,431.46	11/25/2022	$ (2,579)	$ 5,000	$ 2,421
$ 98,313.11	12/25/2022	$ (2,579)	$ 5,000	$ 2,421
$ 96,185.06	1/25/2023	$ (2,579)	$ 5,000	$ 2,421
$ 94,047.25	2/25/2023	$ (2,579)	$ 5,000	$ 2,421
$ 91,899.64	3/25/2023	$ (2,579)	$ 5,000	$ 2,421
$ 89,742.19	4/25/2023	$ (2,579)	$ 5,000	$ 2,421
$ 87,574.85	5/25/2023	$ (2,579)	$ 5,000	$ 2,421
$ 85,397.58	6/25/2023	$ (2,579)	$ 5,000	$ 2,421
$ 83,210.33	7/25/2023	$ (2,579)	$ 5,000	$ 2,421
$ 81,013.05	8/25/2023	$ (2,579)	$ 5,000	$ 2,421
$ 78,805.70	9/25/2023	$ (2,579)	$ 5,000	$ 2,421

Table 10.2 *(continued)* Simple Loan Calculator - Option B

28	10/25/2023	$	78,805.70	$	2,578.66	$	2,217.46	$	361.19
29	11/25/2023	$	76,588.24	$	2,578.66	$	2,227.63	$	351.03
30	12/25/2023	$	74,360.61	$	2,578.66	$	2,237.84	$	340.82
31	1/25/2024	$	72,122.77	$	2,578.66	$	2,248.09	$	330.56
32	2/25/2024	$	69,874.68	$	2,578.66	$	2,258.40	$	320.26
33	3/25/2024	$	67,616.28	$	2,578.66	$	2,268.75	$	309.91
34	4/25/2024	$	65,347.53	$	2,578.66	$	2,279.15	$	299.51
35	5/25/2024	$	63,068.39	$	2,578.66	$	2,289.59	$	289.06
36	6/25/2024	$	60,778.79	$	2,578.66	$	2,300.09	$	278.57
37	7/25/2024	$	58,478.71	$	2,578.66	$	2,310.63	$	268.03
38	8/25/2024	$	56,168.08	$	2,578.66	$	2,321.22	$	257.44
39	9/25/2024	$	53,846.86	$	2,578.66	$	2,331.86	$	246.80
40	10/25/2024	$	51,515.00	$	2,578.66	$	2,342.55	$	236.11
41	11/25/2024	$	49,172.45	$	2,578.66	$	2,353.28	$	225.37
42	12/25/2024	$	46,819.17	$	2,578.66	$	2,364.07	$	214.59
43	1/25/2025	$	44,455.10	$	2,578.66	$	2,374.90	$	203.75
44	2/25/2025	$	42,080.19	$	2,578.66	$	2,385.79	$	192.87
45	3/25/2025	$	39,694.41	$	2,578.66	$	2,396.72	$	181.93
46	4/25/2025	$	37,297.68	$	2,578.66	$	2,407.71	$	170.95
47	5/25/2025	$	34,889.97	$	2,578.66	$	2,418.74	$	159.91
48	6/25/2025	$	32,471.23	$	2,578.66	$	2,429.83	$	148.83
49	7/25/2025	$	30,041.40	$	2,578.66	$	2,440.97	$	137.69
50	8/25/2025	$	27,600.43	$	2,578.66	$	2,452.15	$	126.50
51	9/25/2025	$	25,148.27	$	2,578.66	$	2,463.39	$	115.26
52	10/25/2025	$	22,684.88	$	2,578.66	$	2,474.68	$	103.97
53	11/25/2025	$	20,210.20	$	2,578.66	$	2,486.03	$	92.63
54	12/25/2025	$	17,724.17	$	2,578.66	$	2,497.42	$	81.24
55	1/25/2026	$	15,226.75	$	2,578.66	$	2,508.87	$	69.79
56	2/25/2026	$	12,717.88	$	2,578.66	$	2,520.37	$	58.29
57	3/25/2026	$	10,197.51	$	2,578.66	$	2,531.92	$	46.74
58	4/25/2026	$	7,665.60	$	2,578.66	$	2,543.52	$	35.13
59	5/25/2026	$	5,122.07	$	2,578.66	$	2,555.18	$	23.48
60	6/25/2026	$	2,566.89	$	2,578.66	$	2,566.89	$	11.76

$	76,588.24	10/25/2023	$	(2,579)	$	5,000	$	2,421
$	74,360.61	11/25/2023	$	(2,579)	$	5,000	$	2,421
$	72,122.77	12/25/2023	$	(2,579)	$	5,000	$	2,421
$	69,874.68	1/25/2024	$	(2,579)	$	5,000	$	2,421
$	67,616.28	2/25/2024	$	(2,579)	$	5,000	$	2,421
$	65,347.53	3/25/2024	$	(2,579)	$	5,000	$	2,421
$	63,068.39	4/25/2024	$	(2,579)	$	5,000	$	2,421
$	60,778.79	5/25/2024	$	(2,579)	$	5,000	$	2,421
$	58,478.71	6/25/2024	$	(2,579)	$	5,000	$	2,421
$	56,168.08	7/25/2024	$	(2,579)	$	5,000	$	2,421
$	53,846.86	8/25/2024	$	(2,579)	$	5,000	$	2,421
$	51,515.00	9/25/2024	$	(2,579)	$	5,000	$	2,421
$	49,172.45	10/25/2024	$	(2,579)	$	5,000	$	2,421
$	46,819.17	11/25/2024	$	(2,579)	$	5,000	$	2,421
$	44,455.10	12/25/2024	$	(2,579)	$	5,000	$	2,421
$	42,080.19	1/25/2025	$	(2,579)	$	5,000	$	2,421
$	39,694.41	2/25/2025	$	(2,579)	$	5,000	$	2,421
$	37,297.68	3/25/2025	$	(2,579)	$	5,000	$	2,421
$	34,889.97	4/25/2025	$	(2,579)	$	5,000	$	2,421
$	32,471.23	5/25/2025	$	(2,579)	$	5,000	$	2,421
$	30,041.40	6/25/2025	$	(2,579)	$	5,000	$	2,421
$	27,600.43	7/25/2025	$	(2,579)	$	5,000	$	2,421
$	25,148.27	8/25/2025	$	(2,579)	$	5,000	$	2,421
$	22,684.88	9/25/2025	$	(2,579)	$	5,000	$	2,421
$	20,210.20	10/25/2025	$	(2,579)	$	5,000	$	2,421
$	17,724.17	11/25/2025	$	(2,579)	$	5,000	$	2,421
$	15,226.75	12/25/2025	$	(2,579)	$	5,000	$	2,421
$	12,717.88	1/25/2026	$	(2,579)	$	5,000	$	2,421
$	10,197.51	2/25/2026	$	(2,579)	$	5,000	$	2,421
$	7,665.60	3/25/2026	$	(2,579)	$	5,000	$	2,421
$	5,122.07	4/24/2026	$	(2,579)	$	5,000	$	2,421
$	2,566.89	5/24/2026	$	(2,579)	$	5,000	$	2,421
$	(0.00)	6/23/2026	$	(2,579)	$	5,000	$	2,421

Table 10.3 Simple Loan Calculator - Option C

	Enter values
Loan amount	$150,000.00
Annual interest rate	5.50%
Loan period in years	5.00
Start date of loan	6/25/2021

Monthly payment	$2,865.17
Number of payments	60
Total interest	$21,910.46
Total cost of loan	$171,910.46
NPV	$112,127

No.	Payment Date	Beginning Balance	Payment	Principal	Interest
1	7/25/2021	$ 150,000.00	$ 2,865.17	$ 2,177.67	$ 687.50
2	8/25/2021	$ 147,822.33	$ 2,865.17	$ 2,187.66	$ 677.52
3	9/25/2021	$ 145,634.67	$ 2,865.17	$ 2,197.68	$ 667.49
4	10/25/2021	$ 143,436.99	$ 2,865.17	$ 2,207.75	$ 657.42
5	11/25/2021	$ 141,229.23	$ 2,865.17	$ 2,217.87	$ 647.30
6	12/25/2021	$ 139,011.36	$ 2,865.17	$ 2,228.04	$ 637.14
7	1/25/2022	$ 136,783.32	$ 2,865.17	$ 2,238.25	$ 626.92
8	2/25/2022	$ 134,545.07	$ 2,865.17	$ 2,248.51	$ 616.66
9	3/25/2022	$ 132,296.56	$ 2,865.17	$ 2,258.82	$ 606.36
10	4/25/2022	$ 130,037.75	$ 2,865.17	$ 2,269.17	$ 596.01
11	5/25/2022	$ 127,768.58	$ 2,865.17	$ 2,279.57	$ 527.05
12	6/25/2022	$ 125,489.01	$ 2,865.17	$ 2,290.02	$ 575.16
13	7/25/2022	$ 123,198.99	$ 2,865.17	$ 2,300.51	$ 564.66
14	8/25/2022	$ 120,898.48	$ 2,865.17	$ 2,311.06	$ 554.12
15	9/25/2022	$ 118,587.42	$ 2,865.17	$ 2,321.65	$ 543.53
16	10/25/2022	$ 116,265.78	$ 2,865.17	$ 2,332.29	$ 532.88
17	11/25/2022	$ 113,933.49	$ 2,865.17	$ 2,342.98	$ 522.20
18	12/25/2022	$ 111,590.51	$ 2,865.17	$ 2,353.72	$ 511.46
19	1/25/2023	$ 109,236.79	$ 2,865.17	$ 2,364.51	$ 500.67
20	2/25/2023	$ 106,872.28	$ 2,865.17	$ 2,375.34	$ 489.83
21	3/25/2023	$ 104,496.94	$ 2,865.17	$ 2,386.23	$ 478.94
22	4/25/2023	$ 102,110.71	$ 2,865.17	$ 2,397.17	$ 468.01
23	5/25/2023	$ 99,713.54	$ 2,865.17	$ 2,408.15	$ 457.02
24	6/25/2023	$ 97,305.39	$ 2,865.17	$ 2,419.19	$ 445.98
25	7/25/2023	$ 94,886.20	$ 2,865.17	$ 2,430.28	$ 434.90
26	8/25/2023	$ 92,455.92	$ 2,865.17	$ 2,441.42	$ 423.76
27	9/25/2023	$ 90,014.50	$ 2,865.17	$ 2,452.61	$ 412.57
28	10/25/2023	$ 87,561.89	$ 2,865.17	$ 2,463.85	$ 401.33
29	11/25/2023	$ 85,098.04	$ 2,865.17	$ 2,475.14	$ 390.03

		Pmts only	Positive cash flows	Net cash flows
EndingBalance	6/25/2021	$ (15,000)		$ (15,000)
$ 147,822.33	7/25/2021	$ (2,865)	$ 5,000	$ 2,135
$ 145,634.67	8/25/2021	$ (2,865)	$ 5,000	$ 2,135
$ 143,436.99	9/25/2021	$ (2,865)	$ 5,000	$ 2,135
$ 127,106.31	10/25/2021	$ (2,865)	$ 5,000	$ 2,135
$ 139,011.36	11/25/2021	$ (2,865)	$ 5,000	$ 2,135
$ 136,783.32	12/25/2021	$ (2,865)	$ 5,000	$ 2,135
$ 134,545.07	1/25/2022	$ (2,865)	$ 5,000	$ 2,135
$ 132,296.56	2/25/2022	$ (2,865)	$ 5,000	$ 2,135
$ 130,037.75	3/25/2022	$ (2,865)	$ 5,000	$ 2,135
$ 127,768.5	4/25/2022	$ (2,865)	$ 5,000	$ 2,135
$ 125,489.01	5/25/2022	$ (2,865)	$ 5,000	$ 2,135
$ 123,198.99	6/25/2022	$ (2,865)	$ 5,000	$ 2,135
$ 120,898.48	7/25/2022	$ (2,865)	$ 5,000	$ 2,135
$ 118,587.42	8/25/2022	$ (2,865)	$ 5,000	$ 2,135
$ 116,265.78	9/25/2022	$ (2,865)	$ 5,000	$ 2,135
$ 113,933.49	10/25/2022	$ (2,865)	$ 5,000	$ 2,135
$ 111,590.51	11/25/2022	$ (2,865)	$ 5,000	$ 2,135
$ 109,236.79	12/25/2022	$ (2,865)	$ 5,000	$ 2,135
$ 106,872.28	1/25/2023	$ (2,865)	$ 5,000	$ 2,135
$ 104,496.94	2/25/2023	$ (2,865)	$ 5,000	$ 2,135
$ 102,110.71	3/25/2023	$ (2,865)	$ 5,000	$ 2,135
$ 99,713.54	4/25/2023	$ (2,865)	$ 5,000	$ 2,135
$ 97,305.39	5/25/2023	$ (2,865)	$ 5,000	$ 2,135
$ 94,886.20	6/25/2023	$ (2,865)	$ 5,000	$ 2,135
$ 92,455.92	7/25/2023	$ (2,865)	$ 5,000	$ 2,135
$ 90,014.50	8/25/2023	$ (2,865)	$ 5,000	$ 2,135
$ 87,561.89	9/25/2023	$ (2,865)	$ 5,000	$ 2,135
$ 85,098.04	10/25/2023	$ (2,865)	$ 5,000	$ 2,135
$ 82,622.90	11/25/2023	$ (2,865)	$ 5,000	$ 2,135

Table 10.3 *(continued)* Simple Loan Calculator - Option C

30	12/25/2023	$	82,622.90	$	2,865.17	$	2,486.49	$	378.69
31	1/25/2024	$	80,136.42	$	2,865.17	$	2,497.88	$	367.29
32	2/25/2024	$	77,653 38	$	2,865.17	$	2,509.33	$	355.84
33	3/25/2024	$	75,129.20	$	2,865.17	$	2,520.83	$	344.34
34	4/25/2024	$	72,608.37	$	2,865.17	$	2,279.15	$	332.79
35	5/25/2024	$	70,075.98	$	2,865.17	$	2,543.99	$	321.18
36	6/25/2024	$	67,531.99	$	2,865.17	$	2,555.65	$	309.52
37	7/25/2024	$	64,976.34	$	2,865.17	$	2,567.37	$	297.81
38	8/25/2024	$	62,408.97	$	2,865.17	$	2,579.13	$	286.04
39	9/25/2024	$	59,829.84	$	2,865.17	$	2,590.95	$	274.22
40	10/25/2024	$	57,238.89	$	2,865.17	$	2,602.83	$	262.34
41	11/25/2024	$	54,636.06	$	2,865.17	$	2,614.76	$	250.42
42	12/25/2024	$	52,021.30	$	2,865.17	$	2,626.74	$	238.43
43	1/25/2025	$	49,394.55	$	2,865.17	$	2,638.78	$	226.39
44	2/25/2025	$	46,755.77	$	2,865.17	$	2,650.88	$	214.30
45	3/25/2025	$	44,104.89	$	2,865.17	$	2,663.03	$	202.15
46	4/25/2025	$	41,441.87	$	2,865.17	$	2,675.23	$	189.94
47	5/25/2025	$	38,766.64	$	2,865.17	$	2,687.49	$	177.68
48	6/25/2025	$	36,079.14	$	2,865.17	$	2,699.81	$	165.36
49	7/25/2025	$	33,379.33	$	2,865.17	$	2,712.19	$	152.99
50	8/25/2025	$	30,667.14	$	2,865.17	$	2,724.62	$	140.56
51	9/25/2025	$	27,942.53	$	2,865.17	$	2,737.10	$	128.07
52	10/25/2025	$	25,205.42	$	2,865.17	$	2,749.65	$	115.52
53	11/25/2025	$	22,455.77	$	2,865.17	$	2,762.25	$	102.92
54	12/25/2025	$	19,693.52	$	2,865.17	$	2,774.91	$	90.26
55	1/25/2026	$	16,918.61	$	2,865.17	$	2,787.63	$	77.54
56	2/25/2026	$	14,130.98	$	2,865.17	$	2,800.41	$	64.77
57	3/25/2026	$	11,330.57	$	2,865.17	$	2,813.24	$	51.93
58	4/25/2026	$	8,517.33	$	2,865.17	$	2,826.14	$	39.04
59	5/25/2026	$	5,691.19	$	2,865.17	$	2,839.09	$	26.08
60	6/25/2026	$	2,852.10	$	2,865.17	$	2,852.10	$	13.07

$ 80,136.42	12/25/2023	$ (2,865)	$ 5,000	$ 2,135
$ 77,638.53	1/25/2024	$ (2,865)	$ 5,000	$ 2,135
$ 75,129.20	2/25/2024	$ (2,865)	$ 5,000	$ 2,135
$ 72,608.37	3/25/2024	$ (2,865)	$ 5,000	$ 2,135
$ 70,075.98	4/25/2024	$ (2,865)	$ 5,000	$ 2,135
$ 67,531.99	5/25/2024	$ (2,865)	$ 5,000	$ 2,135
$ 64,976.34	6/25/2024	$ (2,865)	$ 5,000	$ 2,135
$ 62,408.97	7/25/2024	$ (2,865)	$ 5,000	$ 2,135
$ 59,829.84	8/25/2024	$ (2,865)	$ 5,000	$ 2,135
$ 57,238.89	9/25/2024	$ (2,865)	$ 5,000	$ 2,135
$ 54,636.06	10/25/2024	$ (2,865)	$ 5,000	$ 2,135
$ 52,021.30	11/25/2024	$ (2,865)	$ 5,000	$ 2,135
$ 49,394.55	12/25/2024	$ (2,865)	$ 5,000	$ 2,135
$ 46,755.77	1/25/2025	$ (2,865)	$ 5,000	$ 2,135
$ 44,104.89	2/25/2025	$ (2,865)	$ 5,000	$ 2,135
$ 41,441.87	3/25/2025	$ (2,865)	$ 5,000	$ 2,135
$ 38,766.64	4/25/2025	$ (2,865)	$ 5,000	$ 2,135
$ 36,079.14	5/25/2025	$ (2,865)	$ 5,000	$ 2,135
$ 33,379.33	6/24/2025	$ (2,865)	$ 5,000	$ 2,135
$ 30,667.14	7/24/2025	$ (2,865)	$ 5,000	$ 2,135
$ 27,942.53	8/23/2025	$ (2,865)	$ 5,000	$ 2,135
$ 25,205.42	9/22/2025	$ (2,865)	$ 5,000	$ 2,135
$ 22,455.77	10/22/2025	$ (2,865)	$ 5,000	$ 2,135
$ 19,693.52	11/21/2025	$ (2,865)	$ 5,000	$ 2,135
$ 16,918.61	12/21/2025	$ (2,865)	$ 5,000	$ 2,135
$ 14,130.98	1/20/2026	$ (2,865)	$ 5,000	$ 2,135
$ 11,330.57	2/19/2026	$ (2,865)	$ 5,000	$ 2,135
$ 8,517.33	3/21/2026	$ (2,865)	$ 5,000	$ 2,135
$ 5,691.19	4/20/2026	$ (2,865)	$ 5,000	$ 2,135
$ 2,852.10	5/20/2026	$ (2,865)	$ 5,000	$ 2,135
$ (0.00)	6/19/2026	$ (2,865)	$ 5,000	$ 2,135

of any individual who owns 20% or more of the company and/or who is key to operations.

When preparing financial reports for a lender, make sure that you are providing accurate data on an accrual basis. Present at least two years of financials. If you are presenting pro forma financials or projections present the most likely scenario.

ALTERNATIVE FINANCING OPTIONS

Aside from alternative lenders, there are other alternative ways to finance a company outside of traditional debt and equity.

Hybrid debt-equity

This model requires investors to contribute equal amounts debt and equity. For example, to get $10,000 equity, an investor would be required to lend an equal amount of debt. The benefit to a business of a hybrid model is that a founder gets double the cash for the amount of equity that is sold. The drawback is that it adds debt to the balance sheet.

Convertible debt

Convertible debt is a loan that has the possibility of turning to equity at some point in the future. The benefit to business owners is access cash at a lower cost of capital than institutional debt. Also, convertible debtholders do not have voting rights in an organization. The drawback to the company is that existing equity holders may be diluted in the future if the debt converts to equity.

Put options

Put options are attached to traditional equity. The put option mitigates risk for investors, and therefore might make capital more accessible to a distillery. An individual may be more apt to contribute cash if there is an option to get it back later if he decides he wants out. The put option allows an investor to exercise the right some or all equity back to the company at a designated price. If a company cannot fully repay the investor when the put is exercised, the unpaid amount becomes debt and is paid back with interest.

Crowdfunding

Crowdfunding involves taking on funds from several (sometimes hundreds of) small investors. The fundraising is usually facilitated through an online platform. Usually, the company receiving the money gives donors some token, such as a piece of merchandise. Money received is taxable; it is treated as revenue.

Line of credit

A business line of credit is short term debt usually funded through a bank. A line of credit should be used if a bridge of cash is needed to get through a slow season. It is common for a line of credit to be required to rest at $0 for a period of at least 30 consecutive days each year.

Home equity line of credit

Home equity line of credit (HELOC). A HELOC is funded through a bank or real estate lender and allows an individual to borrow cash. The amount borrowed is tied to the amount of equity the individual has in his or her home. In a business context, the individual borrows the money personally, then contributes it to the business. One benefit is that the money is not taxable and does not add to debt on the company's balance sheet; it is considered an owner equity contribution, not debt. A drawback is that the owner has now put a major personal asset (the home) in a risky position because the ability to pay back the home equity line of credit is dependent on the performance of the business.

Investment account loans

Some brokerage funds, and even retirement plans, offer loans against the assets in the account. This, like a home equity line of credit, is a risky option because it ties personal assets to business performance.

AUTHOR'S NOTE: I strongly encourage all owners to avoid personal debt as a source of financing for a business expansion.

Grants

Many governmental agencies offer grants to distilleries. Grants are used to incentivize government goals, such as economic revitalization of a certain geography, or increases to employment. Grants are also available in many regions to minority owned businesses.

From a thirty thousand foot view, it is true that financing comes in two forms: debt or equity. Fortunately, within those categories there are a multitude of options. Thinking outside the box and doing a bit of research can open the door to many financing options beyond the usual suspects.

FINANCE OPTIONS FOR EXPANSION

The production facility is bound by physical limitations that are built to serve a certain range of production — the relevant range. A facility might be built for a capacity of 20,000 proof gallons. When production demand exceeds the capacity of a facility, a company is forced to meet the demand by expanding capacity in some way, or limiting sales to only what can be produced within the existing footprint. A change in relevant range means an increase in costs. Expanded capacity may be created by building a new facility, engaging in a contract manufacturing agreement, or streamlining to a more efficient production process.

The efficiency of equipment is another limitation that may force a producer to purchase new and better equipment that allows more product to be pushed through the same square footage. As equipment ages, the cost of producing goods creeps up with other costs such as maintenance. A facility that uses separate pieces of equipment to complete one job is inherently less efficient than one full unit. For example, a canning line with multiple disjointed pieces will not be as productive as a robust one-unit line. Production facility engineering can also increase efficiency. Before moving forward with an expansion, consider it from all angles. This section includes several points to consider before taking action on a expansion.

Capacity considerations:

- What size batches are being produced?
- How does that compare to the size of equipment?
- If equipment is underutilized, could the batch size be increased, and therefore less frequent production runs would be required for a particular product?
- Does the product have the shelf life to sustain additional time on the warehouse floor?
- Is there sufficient storage area in the warehouse to store the product?
- Could smaller batches be produced more frequently to achieve the needed production?
- How would these changes affect labor cost?
- If cost goes up, will the market accept a higher shelf price so that margins can stay at the same level?

Capacity is tied to the production process. Consider:

- How many different products are made in the distillery and how much time is needed between changing products that are in production?
- What is the production time for each product?
- How efficient is your equipment?
- How frequently do you replace equipment?
- How long do units sit idle in the production process?
- Are there any activities in the production process that do not add value?

Inventory

- What is the shelf life of your product?
- How much warehouse space is available for storing inventory?
- How many units of inventory are on hand?
- How much is it worth?
- How long do items stay in inventory?
- In what quantity do you purchase raw materials?

Customers

- How much lead time do you have between a customer placing an order and order shipment?
- Does the customer require a minimum shelf life from FOB?
- Or from their distribution center?
- Do you sell large quantities of few products, or small quantities of many products?
- Do customers order consistently or erratically?

PRODUCTION PLANNING

Production planning systems range from a white board on the low-tech end of the scale, to a manufacturing resource planning software on the high-tech end of the scale. Usually, the more mature and larger an organization is, the better production planning system is used. Robust ERP (enterprise resource planning) software can cost tens of thousands of dollars, so it's understandable that smaller organizations may choose to invest capital in other areas of the business. One of the benefits of a well-developed production planning software is that it allows a producer to organize production in the most efficient way possible.

Production planning considerations:

- How much space is available for tote/barrel storage?
- In what order are different products distilled?
- What is the turn time for each product?
- Are special additives or other unique ingredients needed (flavoring, infusing) that require labor or equipment unique to a specific process?

These questions point to considerations for how your production facility should be designed in order to maximize capacity and efficiency. If a company is experiencing capacity restraints, then it may be nearing the upper end of the relevant range for the products' cost structure. Meaning that, if a second facility is required to increase capacity, then additional costs will be added to COGS: rent, utilities, new equipment. As fixed costs increase, the contribution margin of products decrease, and that may put a company at risk of no longer being profitable. Before expanding physical space, consider making adjustments to the current facility that would allow for increased capacity without having to jump into a whole new relevant range of costs. In other words, maximize the current space before building anew.

If upgrading an existing facility, there will undoubtedly be costs associated with some items (for example, buying a faster bottling line), but the dollars will be small compared to what it would cost to build a brand new facility.

Production expansion may be small or large in scope. By considering all options, business owners are positioned to make the smartest decision for the future of the company, and finance the project with the most efficient source of capital.

CHAPTER **ELEVEN**

Preparing for Year-End

Year-end can be exhausting for accounting professionals. There's the rush to close the books, issue 1099s, distribute W2s, and coordinate the preparation of the tax return with your CPA. I am a CPA specializing in craft beverage and have had the opportunity to serve as an external CPA to producers, as well as serve as an outsourced CFO. After seeing both sides of the year-end crunch here are some suggestions for making end of year as painless as possible.

ROLL RETAINED EARNINGS

One of the first things a tax preparer will do is compare book retained earnings for last year (e.g., 12/31/21) to the tax return for the same period. Before closing the books, confirm that retained earnings is the same as the retained earnings balance on the last filed return. Common reasons for a discrepancy include not booking adjusting journal entries that your CPA provided with the prior year return or making changes to transactions in a prior year. By taking the time to ensure retained earnings rolls, the company will save tax preparer time (which of course saves money).

If retained earnings *should* be different than what is on the tax return — due to correction of an error - and if the amount is material, discuss this with your CPA. It may be necessary to file an amended return.

It is important for the books to agree to the tax return because items of income and deduction are reported in the year they are incurred. If history has been changed due to changes you make on the books, the tax result will be different. This can get a company in trouble if it is audited.

AUTHOR'S NOTE:* *This is a common issue that is costly because the tax preparer spends time to get retained earnings to match what was on the previous year's return. This can easily be avoided by (1) not making any changes to the books for a prior year after the data has been given to the CPA to begin tax prep, and (2) booking any adjusting journal entries provided by the CPA after the return has been completed. After adjusting journal entries are booked, the balance sheet per book should agree with the balance sheet as presented on Schedule L of the tax return. If the balance sheet does not agree, contact your CPA for assistance.

REVIEW ALL OPEN TRANSACTIONS

Good year-end housekeeping includes a review of open transactions to make sure only truly outstanding items are showing *Open* status as of 12/31. The Accounting department should check that all sales orders have been closed, all deliveries have been invoiced, and all A/R invoices marked paid, as appropriate. The Purchasing Department should ensure all purchase orders and inventory receipts have been booked and closed. The Production Department should certify that all open production orders have been closed, and all batches in process have been closed.

PROVIDING INFORMATION TO YOUR TAX PREPARER

Before beginning preparation of a return most CPAs provide a list of requested items to the client. Be prepared to provide a copy of your comparative Profit and Loss Statement and Balance Sheet (eg, 2019 vs 2020) in Excel. Also provide a supporting document for each account on the balance sheet. Also include copies of any legal agreements that affect the prior year.

When preparing returns, CPAs build a folder of source documents that support the tax return. Many of these documents will come from the client. Examples include bank, credit card, and loan statements; promissory notes and amortization schedules for any private party loans; A/R and A/P aging reports; inventory audit report; and a detail of changes to fixed assets with description of purchases. Examples of relevant legal documents are subscription agreements for new members added within the year; copy of amended operating agreement; and an updated cap table. By collecting these and submitting with your balance sheet and income statement, you reduce the amount of time that the CPA will spend sending follow-up questions to you.

AUTHOR'S NOTE:* *In my experience I have found that as a preparer, when I have to pick up and put down a return while waiting on additional information from the client, it dramatically effects my efficiency, which of course results in a higher expense for the client.

TAX STRATEGY

Communication with your CPA is an important element of getting optimal tax results. Many business owners are averse to scheduling meetings with a CPA because it is expensive and seen as unnecessary. However, in my experience the benefits are more than worth the extra time and effort. When a CPA is attuned to a company's activities, he or she can work proactively to achieve the best tax result.

How should distillery owners think about the CPA-distillery relationship? Finding the right CPA is like finding the right doctor. They need to be competent, understand you, have good communication skills, and be comfortable for you to work with. Communicate. Talk to them minimum quarterly.

Have a call with your CPA in November to get an estimate of the taxable income you can expect for the year. Once this is known, consider different strategies to reduce tax. The most common tactic is to buy equipment and place it in service before the end of the year so that it can be written off as a tax deduction. Don't blindly spend money on equipment to get additional depreciation. Make sure purchases are well-founded. Minimizing taxes is important, but don't let the tax tail wag the dog. That is, tax management should not come at the expense of a solid financial foundation. Never put a company in a cash poor position to avoid paying tax. This is cutting off your nose to spite your face.

When accelerated depreciation is the chosen method to drive down taxable income a company can get into a cycle in which it can no longer continue to purchase new assets each year. Once this occurs, there is no more accelerated depreciation to reduce the tax burden. While depreciation can seem like a magic bullet for tax planning, once it runs out, the results can be unpleasant at best.

Consider other avenues to reduce taxable income such as retirement plan contributions and research and development credits. These tactics are sustainable because most companies can take advantage of them each year. And, in the case of retirement plan contributions, are an employee benefit that will also contribute to employee satisfaction. It's a win-win.

***AUTHOR'S NOTE:** My advice is that there is no quick fix for taxes. Paying taxes is a good problem to have and an indication that a business is healthy. I wholeheartedly believe in smart tax planning, but it shouldn't be the end goal for your financial picture. Accept that you will owe tax and plan for the cash flow impacts. Be prepared to pay tax distributions or tax payments. Don't wait until the last minute to know where the cash is going to come from.*

Planning for tax payments is an important part of cash flow management. Additionally, money should be set aside for slow months. Most beverage alcohol companies' slow quarters are Q4 and Q1. To prepare for lean months, calculate your cash burn and stow away at least 3 months of operating expenses before slow season starts.

***AUTHOR'S NOTE:** Common Tax Credits for Distilleries*

R&D — Research and Development Credit

Employer Tips Credit

Distilled Spirits Credit

TAX DISTRIBUTIONS

If a company is a flow through entity (a partnership or a S corp) it may be required to issue tax distributions or dividends in the event that it generates taxable income. This depends on the policy defined in the company's governing document. Many operating agreements include a clause that requires tax distributions to be paid to investors. The tax distribution is paid to cover tax liability investors may incur from company income allocated on the K-1. A tax distribution is not characterized differently from an income distribution. In other words, both types of distributions are a return of capital to investors, not income. All distributions deplete capital accounts.

The distinction between a tax distribution versus an income distribution is important because some operating agreements include specific language instructing the order in which distributions occur. For example, a common operating agreement clause states that all investors who provided initial capital for the business will be paid back before sweat equity partners can participate in distributions. However, tax distributions are usually allowed for all investors, even if he or she would not be allowed an income distribution yet. Read the operating agreement and understand the obligations for issuing distributions. This could significantly affect cash flow, and most certainly would be an unwelcomed surprise.

1099s

1099s are due to recipients by January 31 and to the IRS by February 28. As a reminder, 1099s should be issued to all service providers to whom you have paid over $600 in the year and who are *not* incorporated (S corps, C corps). All landlords and attorneys receive a 1099 for rent payments or legal services, respectively, regardless of how much they have been paid or corporate structure.

I recommend collecting vendor W9s throughout the year, and for convenience you can attach the W9 to the Vendor Profile in your accounting system. A best practice is to require the W9 on file before paying a new vendor.

To quote Stephen Covey, "begin with the end in mind" for a successful year-end. Anticipate questions from the CPA to save yourself time and money. With a little organization, the inevitable chaos of the year-end hustle can be tamed!

CHAPTER **TWELVE**

Appendix

SAMPLE CHART OF ACCOUNTS

Number	Account	Type
1000	Checking #1234	Bank
1010	Checking #2345	Bank
1020	Cash on Hand	Bank
1100	Accounts Receivable	Accounts Receivable
1200	Credit Cards Receivable	Other Current Asset
1300	Inventory	Other Current Asset
1310	Inventory:Finished Goods	Other Current Asset
1312	Inventory:Finished Goods:Cases Packaged	Other Current Asset
1314	Inventory:Finished Goods:Kegs	Other Current Asset
1320	Inventory:Merchandise	Other Current Asset
1330	Inventory:Other	Other Current Asset
1340	Inventory:Packaging Materials	Other Current Asset
1350	Inventory:Prepaid Inventory	Other Current Asset
1360	Inventory:Raw Materials	Other Current Asset
1370	Inventory:Tasting Room Inventory	Other Current Asset
1372	Inventory:Tasting Room Inventory:Beer	Other Current Asset
1374	Inventory:Tasting Room Inventory:Food	Other Current Asset
1376	Inventory:Tasting Room Inventory:Guest Spirits	Other Current Asset
1378	Inventory:Tasting Room Inventory:In-House Spirits	Other Current Asset
1380	Inventory:Tasting Room Inventory:Kegged Cocktails	Other Current Asset
1382	Inventory:Tasting Room Inventory:N/A Beverages	Other Current Asset
1384	Inventory:Tasting Room Inventory:Wine	Other Current Asset
1390	Inventory:Work in Process	Other Current Asset
1392	Inventory:Work in Process:Barrel-Aging	Other Current Asset
1400	Prepaid Advertising	Other Current Asset
1500	Undeposited Funds	Other Current Asset
1700	Artwork	Fixed Asset
1710	Goodwill	Other Asset
1790	Accumulated Amortization	Fixed Asset
1800	Building	Fixed Asset
1810	Computer	Fixed Asset
1820	Distillery Equipment	Fixed Asset
1830	Leasehold Improvements	Fixed Asset
1840	Start-up costs	Fixed Asset
1850	Tasting Room Equipment	Fixed Asset
1852	Tasting Room Equipment:Computers	Fixed Asset
1854	Tasting Room Equipment:Equipment	Fixed Asset
1856	Tasting Room Equipment:Furniture and Fixtures	Fixed Asset

Number	Account	Type
1860	Trademark	Fixed Asset
1870	Vehicles	Fixed Asset
1880	Assets Not Yet In Service	Other Asset
1890	Accumulated Depreciation	Fixed Asset
1900	Rent Deposit	Other Asset
2000	Accounts Payable	Accounts Payable
2100	Credit Card	Credit Card
2110	First Bank CC #3456	Credit Card
2120	First Bank CC #4567	Credit Card
2210	Accrued Federal Excise Tax	Other Current Liability
2220	Accrued Interest Payable	Other Current Liability
2230	Deferred Rent	Other Current Liability
2240	Equipment Lease	Other Current Liability
2250	Event Deposits	Other Current Liability
2260	Freight-Out Payable	Other Current Liability
2270	Gift Card Liability	Other Current Liability
2280	Line of Credit	Other Current Liability
2290	Non-Inventory Payable	Other Current Liability
2300	Notes Payable	Other Current Liability
2310	Pallet Deposits	Other Current Liability
2320	Payroll Liabilities	Other Current Liability
2330	Private Party Loan	Other Current Liability
2340	Sales Tax Payable	Other Current Liability
2350	Tips Payable	Other Current Liability
2400	Bank Loans	Long Term Liability
2410	First Bank #6789	Long Term Liability
2420	Frist Bank #5678	Long Term Liability
2430	Loans Payable	Long Term Liability
2432	Loans Payable:SBA Loan	Long Term Liability
3000	Members Equity	Equity
3010	Members Distribution	Equity
4000	Spirits Sales	Income
4002	Spirits Sales:Vodka	Income
4004	Spirits Sales:Gin	Income
4006	Spirits Sales:Whiskey	Income
4010	Food Sales	Income
4020	Beer Sales	Income
4030	Merchandise Sales	Income
4040	N/A Beverage Sales	Income
4050	Wine Sales	Income

Number	Account	Type
4060	Room Rental	Income
4090	Discounts	Income
5000	Spirits COGS	Cost of Goods Sold
5002	Spirits COGS:Vodka	Cost of Goods Sold
5004	Spirits COGS:Gin	Cost of Goods Sold
5006	Spirits COGS:Whiskey	Cost of Goods Sold
5010	Food COGS	Cost of Goods Sold
5020	Beer COGS	Cost of Goods Sold
5030	Merchandise COGS	Cost of Goods Sold
5040	N/A Beverage COGS	Cost of Goods Sold
5050	Wine COGS	Cost of Goods Sold
5060	Depreciation Expense (COGS)	Cost of Goods Sold
5070	Excise Tax	Cost of Goods Sold
5080	Shipping & Delivery	Cost of Goods Sold
5100	Production Payroll	Cost of Goods Sold
6000	Bad Debt	Expense
6010	Bank Service Charges	Expense
6020	Cash Under/Over	Expense
6030	Charitable Contributions	Expense
6040	Computer and Internet Expenses	Expense
6050	Dues and Subscriptions	Expense
6060	Employee Benefits	Expense
6070	Equipment Rental	Expense
6080	Fines and Penalties	Expense
6090	Guaranteed Payment	Expense
6100	Hiring Expenses	Expense
6110	Insurance Expense	Expense
6112	Insurance Expense:General Liability Insurance	Expense
6114	Insurance Expense:Worker's Compensation	Expense
6120	Janitorial Expense	Expense
6130	Lab Supplies	Expense
6140	Landscaping	Expense
6150	Licenses & Permits	Expense
6160	Marketing	Expense
6162	Marketing:Advertising	Expense
6164	Marketing:Advertising:Events	Expense
6166	Marketing:Advertising:Traditional Advertising	Expense
6168	Marketing:Billbacks	Expense
6170	Marketing:Festivals and Awards	Expense
6172	Marketing:Online Sales Revenue Share	Expense

Number	Account	Type
6174	Marketing:Point of Sale Materials	Expense
6180	Merchant Fees	Expense
6190	Office Supplies	Expense
6200	Payroll	Expense
6202	Payroll:Bonuses	Expense
6204	Payroll:Manager Salaries	Expense
6206	Payroll:Payroll Taxes	Expense
6210	Payroll Service Fee	Expense
6220	Postage and Delivery	Expense
6230	Professional Fees	Expense
6232	Professional Fees:Accounting	Expense
6234	Professional Fees:Consulting	Expense
6236	Professional Fees:Legal Fees	Expense
6238	Professional Fees:Marketing	Expense
6240	Professional Fees:Other	Expense
6250	Reference Materials	Expense
6260	Rent Expense	Expense
6262	Rent Expense:Raw Materials Storage Fee	Expense
6270	Repairs and Maintenance	Expense
6280	Sales Expense	Expense
6282	Sales Expense:Automobile Expense	Expense
6284	Sales Expense:Cell Phone	Expense
6286	Sales Expense:Entertainment	Expense
6288	Sales Expense:Meals	Expense
6290	Sales Expense:Parking	Expense
6292	Sales Expense:Samples	Expense
6294	Sales Expense:Travel	Expense
6296	Sales Expense:Travel:Meals	Expense
6300	Small Equipment	Expense
6310	Small Wares	Expense
6320	Supplies	Expense
6322	Supplies:Brewery Supplies	Expense
6324	Supplies:Brewery Supplies:Chemicals	Expense
6326	Supplies:Brewery Supplies:Packaging	Expense
6328	Supplies:Brewery Supplies:Pallets	Expense
6330	Supplies:Brewery Supplies:Safety Supplies	Expense
6332	Supplies:Tasting Room Supplies	Expense
6340	Suspense	Expense
6350	Tasting Room Labor	Expense
6352	Tasting Room Labor:Back of House Labor	Expense

Number	Account	Type
6354	Tasting Room Labor:Front of House Labor	Expense
6360	Taxes	Expense
6362	Taxes:Local	Expense
6364	Taxes:Property Taxes	Expense
6366	Taxes:State	Expense
6370	Telephone/Cable/Internet	Expense
6380	Theft Loss	Other Expense
6390	Uniforms	Expense
6400	Utilities	Expense
6402	Utilities:Garbage Service	Expense
6404	Utilities:Natural Gas	Expense
6406	Utilities:Power	Expense
6408	Utilities:Security	Expense
6410	Utilities:Water	Expense
6420	Waste	Expense
6500	Depreciation Expense (Non-COGS)	Expense
6510	Amortization	Expense
7000	Distributor Bonus	Other Income
7010	Gain/Loss on Sale of Equipment	Other Income
7020	Insurance Proceeds	Other Income
7030	Interest Income	Other Income
8000	Other Income	Other Income
8010	Interest Expense	Other Expense

MONTH-END CLOSE TEMPLATE

CASH
Reconcile bank accounts. Verify bank balance on reconciliation report agrees with bank balance on statement.
Review outstanding checks and deposits for old transactions that need to be voided.

UNDEPOSITED FUNDS
Balance in account should be reconciled to deposits clearing in the next month.
Verify all undeposited funds from a prior month clear in the current month.

ACCOUNTS RECEIVABLE
Review accounts receivable aging report and verify that the total agrees with trial balance.
Determine if any past due balances need to be written off.
Review the aging report for outstanding customer credits that need to be applied to open A/R.

INVENTORY
Complete a hard count of inventory by comparing quantities on hand to quantities in the inventory management system. Prepare and post adjustment if necessary.
Review inventory subledger for manual adjustments.
Review the average cost per unit of inventory items, scanning for anomalies that may need to be reviewed.
Determine if any obsolete inventory exists that needs to be written off.

FIXED ASSETS
Identify fixed asset additions and disposals during the period and document acquisition/disposal date and asset description.
If an asset is sold, record the disposal of the asset, reduction to accumulated depreciation, and any gain or loss.
Reconcile balance sheet account balances for fixed assets and accumulated depreciation to the depreciation schedule.
Record depreciation and amortization expense for the period.

RECONCILE INTERCOMPANY ACCOUNTS
Verify intercompany payables and receivables have the same balance in each entity's books.

PREPAID EXPENSES
Verify balances agree to a supporting schedule and can be traced to payments made.
Record monthly recognition of expenses to reduce prepaid expenses.

NOTES RECEIVABLE
Verify ending account balance agrees with the related loan amortization schedule.

ACCOUNTS PAYABLE
Review accounts payable aging report and verify that the total agrees with the trial balance.
Review the aging report for outstanding vendor credits that need to be applied to open A/P.

PAYROLL LIABILITIES
Trace the balance in account to supporting payroll records for the respective month.
Determine the correct amount of days' pay in the accrual when calculating liability.

PAYROLL TAX LIABILITIES
Trace the balance of the account to the payroll tax returns filed in the following month, or to tax payments made in the following month for a current month payroll.

ACCRUED PROPERTY TAX
Verify the monthly accrual is equal to 1/12 the anticipated expense for the current year.

ACCRUED SALES TAX
Verify the balance in the liability account agrees to respective sales tax reports filed in the following month.

NOTES PAYABLE
Reconcile balance to amortization schedule or statement that supports the note. Determine if monthly interest expense has been properly recorded.

EQUITY
Verify that any personal expenses of an owner have been properly recorded in the drawing account, or in an owner receivable account.
Verify all changes to equity accounts are correctly recorded.
Verify that retained earnings or capital accounts agree with balances on prior year tax return.

INCOME
If using separate software (e.g., POS software for a tasting room or inventory management software), run a sales summary report and confirm that income reported in the period agrees with the sum of sales from other software.
Verify that all sales are appropriately recorded in the correct income account.

EXPENSES
Review the detail of the following accounts to verify proper classification: repairs, supplies, meals, travel, miscellaneous expense.
Scan general ledger to verify accuracy of entry classification in other accounts.

GLOSSARY

Account ledger a collection of transactions that have been assigned to a particular account.

Accounting transaction the smallest unit of the accounting language. In each transaction there are two sides: a debit and a credit, and each side must balance the other.

Accrual basis accounting recognizes revenue and expenses in the period incurred, regardless of when cash is disbursed or received.

Asset a resource owned by an entity with an expected future economic benefit.

Asset turnover the value of a company's sales or revenues generated relative to the value of its assets. A higher number is better.

B corporation a new kind of business that balances purpose and profit. They are legally required to consider the impact of their decisions on their workers, customers, suppliers, community, and the environment.[1]

Balance sheet a financial report that shows the financial status of an entity at a moment in time. It is composed of assets, liabilities, and equity.

Basis of accounting a system that determines when transactions and events are recorded on a company's books.

Bill of materials a list of all materials required to manufacture a product.

Bookkeeper party responsible for recording transactions into the company's accounting system. The bookkeeper normally records sales, purchases, payroll data, and other operating expenses.

Break-even expressed in dollars or in units, break-even is the point at which all expenses for a period have been covered. With each successive sale net income is created.

Business model a structure for business operations.

C corporation a business structure that is not a flow-through entity. Corporations are deemed to be an independent entity and pay their own taxes. Ownership in C corporations is expressed in shares.

Capex abbreviated term for capital expenses.

Capital budgeting the process used to evaluate a major investment. Generally, it involves analyzing a project's long term cash flows and calculation of return on investment versus the hurdle rate.

Capitalize to include an expense in the cost of an asset.

Capitalization policy a threshold dollar amount set by a company, over which a purchase will be capitalized, and under which a purchase will be expensed.

Cash basis accounting recognizes revenue when cash is received and recognizes expenses when cash is disbursed.

Cash conversion cycle the amount of time between spending a dollar on an expense to the point where the dollar appears as profit on sales.

Cash flow statement One of the three reports that comprise a complete set of financial reports. The cash flow statement is the link between the balance sheet and the income statement. It shows the sources and uses of cash over a period of time.

Cash flow forecast a management tool that identifies projected low points of cash and aids in strategic planning.

1 www.bcorporation.net

Chart of accounts a list of accounts in a company's general ledger.

CFO (Chief Financial Officer) the individual responsible for leading long-term, sustainable financial success of a company. The CFO links owners' or Board of Directors' objectives to the business operations. The CFO analyzes data and provides recommendations that enable the leadership team to make decisions.

Collateral something of value pledged as security for repayment of a loan.

Compound interest interest calculation in which the interest rate is multiplied by the sum of the principal *plus* the accumulated interest of previous periods. Compounding periods can be any set amount of time, and generally will be annually, quarterly, monthly, or daily.

Contribution margin sales price per unit minus variable costs per unit.

Controller Individual in an accounting department responsible for the development and implementation of the accounting system. He or she may supervise bookkeepers or other accounting department staff. The Controller is often responsible for setting internal controls.

Convertible debt a loan that has the possibility of turning to equity at some point in the future.

Cost accounting a method of accounting used internally by management to determine all costs associated with a product or line of business.

Cost of capital the required return on investment to make a project worthwhile. Capital may be comprised of debt, equity, or both. Cost of capital is a blended rate of both components, also known as weighted average cost of capital. This is often referred to by its acronym, WACC.

Cost of goods sold total of all costs incurred to create a product or service that has been sold.

Crowdfunding a form of financing in which funds are collected from several (sometimes hundreds of) small investors. The fundraising is often facilitated through an online platform.

Current asset asset expected to be sold or used within the next twelve months.

Current liability liability expected to be paid within the next twelve months.

Current ratio A financial metric that measures liquidity. It is calculated as current assets divided by current liabilities.

Days sales inventory a calculation of the number of days of sales a company could fill with the current inventory level. It is calculated as average inventory / COGS * 365.

Days sales outstanding the average number of days it takes for a company to collect payment for a sale.

Debt service coverage a measure of a company's available cash to pay debt obligations.

Debt to equity a financial metric that measures leverage. It is calculated as total liabilities divided by total equity.

Depreciation an method used to allocate the cost of a fixed asset over its useful life.

Discounted Cash Flow Analysis A method for measuring a project's projected return that accounts for initial costs, expected inflows, and ongoing costs.

EBITDA a measure of a company's profitability. It is calculated as earnings plus interest expense plus taxes plus depreciation and amortization.

Equity represents the amount of money that would be paid to company owners if all assets were liquidated and all debts were settled.

Fixed costs expenses that stay the same over a period of time or relevant range and which do not change with the level of production.

Flow-through entity a type of organizational structure in which there no entity-level income tax. All tax items are taxed on the underlying individual's tax return.

FOB an acronym for freight on board. This indicates when liability of a product shifts from one party to another. In the context of beverage alcohol sales, FOB refers to the sales price of a good from a supplier to a wholesaler.

General ledger combines all of the individual account ledgers and is presented in order of account type.

GAAP short for Generally Accepted Accounting Principles, GAAP are standards for corporate accounting.

Grant a financial award given to incentivize performance or to facilitate a goal. Usually grants do not need to be repaid.

Gross Margin net sales minus cost of goods sold.

Hurdle rate the required return that a project must meet before being approved by company leadership.

Income statement shows the performance of a business over a period of time.

Interest rate the percentage rate charged for the use of assets.

Internal controls processes and procedures that mitigate the risk of fraudulent acts.

Inventory turnover a calculation of how many times a company's inventory is sold and replaced over a period of time. A low turnover implies excess inventory and/or room to improve sales. A high ratio implies either strong sales and/or large discounts.

Labor efficiency measures how much profit is generated by each dollar of labor.

Lagging indicator an observable or measurable factor that changes after the business variable with which it is correlated changes.

Leading indicator an observable or measurable factor that changes before the business variable with which it is correlated changes.

Liability A liability is an obligation to pay in the future.

Liquidity a company's ability to pay obligations as they come due.

Loss leader a product sold at a loss to attract customers.

Margin the sales price of an item less COGS.

Mark-up the percentage increase added to the cost of a good.

Net income revenue minus all expenses.

Net operating income revenue minus COGS and all operating expenses. Net operating income does not include other income or expenses not related to ordinary operations.

Net present value (NPV) the current value of future cash flows from an investment.

Noncurrent asset asset expected to be sold or used at some point after the next twelve months.

Noncurrent liability liability expected to be paid after the next twelve months.

Open book management the business practice of creating transparency by sharing financial information with employees.

Partnership a business structure in which two or more persons or entities collectively own a business.

Payback analysis a method for measuring a project's projected return that measures how long it will take to recoup the initial investment.

Personal guarantee an individual's legal promise to repay credit extended to a business.

Profit and loss statement see Income Statement

Put option an option attached to equity that allows an investor to exercise the right to have the company buy back his equity.

Quick ratio a financial metric that measures liquidity. It is calculated as the sum of all liquid and near liquid assets divided by current liabilities.

Relevant range a specific activity level that is bounded by a minimum and maximum amount.

Retained earnings a company's cumulative earnings after accounting for distributions.

Risk-return tradeoff the concept that the potential return of an investment is inversely correlated to its risk.

S corporation a business structure in which a corporation elects to be taxed as a small business corporation. Tax characteristics flow-through to the underlying individual owners.

Simple interest interest calculation in which the daily interest rate is multiplied by the principal and again multiplied by the number of days between payments.

Single member LLC a business structure in which the entity is owned by one party. The entity is shielded by an LLC envelope to provide certain legal protections.

Sole proprietorship the simplest business organization form. It is run by only one person under his own name or a trade name. There is no formal entity to designate the assets of the business from the assets of the owner.

Statement of cash flows a financial statement that summarizes the sources and uses of cash of a company over a period of time.

Throughput analysis a method for measuring a project's projected return that considers how the investment will affect the organization as a whole.

Time value of money the concept that money decreases in value over time due to its earning capacity, which relates to inflation.

Value stream the chain of events that create value for a customer while producing a product.

Variable costs an expense that changes proportionally to how much a company produces or sells.

CPSIA information can be obtained
at www.ICGtesting.com
Printed in the USA
LVHW062033220822
726418LV00011B/204